IMPROVEMENT STARTS WITH I

A PRACTICAL GUIDE TO BUILDING AN EXTRAORDINARY **LEAN** CULTURE

TOM HUGHES

Feel free to connect with Tom, just scan a QR code!

Please use Voxer, Signal or WhatsApp rather than email for any messages!

V-card

CONTENTS

ACKNOWLEDGEMENTS

This could easily be the longest section of the book, but we are practising lean, so it's not going to be!

I consider myself fortunate to have come on to this path of personal growth and development. So many of the people I have come into contact with in the lean world have grown from acquaintances into good buddies and occasionally real friends – a word I don't use lightly.

My first thanks go to Mr Paul Akers for starting this whole world of 2 Second Lean, writing the book, giving tirelessly to myself and the world in a way that is not for "1 Second" (pardon the pun!) for personal gain. I am so lucky to count him as a true friend and the best mentor one could wish for.

To Alex Ramirez, Steven Pax, Brannon Burton, and Andries Overweg for being my initial editors and significant contributors to the material. Thank you so much for taking the time and effort to do so and for being direct enough with your critiques but kind enough with your support to make that whole process so productive and fun.

To Ryan Tierney and all at Seating Matters, especially JB, Declan, and Alison who, as well as being amazing examples of what is possible in our little country of Ireland, took the time to support other companies, as you have supported me, on our lean path.

To Paul Vallely at Kukoon Rugs, who has also been so supportive in my early days of 2 Second Lean and in pretty much all my recent endeavours, including becoming an early adopter of GembaDocs. Thanks for your friendship and all your help. It is much appreciated.

To Patrick Magee, my friend and business partner who is just a joy to know and work with. We have the same values but different approaches, and that is why 1 + 1 equals a lot more than 2. I am looking forward to building a true beacon of excellence with you, sir.

To Dave Lelonek for being a great, fun, right leaning friend and starting the Lean Maniacs Signal Group. Every day is an inspiration being part of that community, and I grow so much for the exposure to all those real Lean Maniacs. My sincere thanks to all of them too.

To my beautiful partner, Fiona, for having the patience to listen to me rave on about my latest satori moment of realisation while I have been writing this book and just being my closest and most intimate life partner. You are one of the reasons I thank God every day for being here.

To my family, Tiernan, Dylan, Cara, and soon-to-be step-daughter, Bevin, thanks for having the courage to be yourselves because that is not easy these days. Thanks also for contributing to all the love in my life. There is a lot of it.

To all my great friends and former colleagues mentioned in the book, thanks for being there and making life as fun and as interesting as it has been so far!

Finally, to God and my guru, Paramahansa Yogananda, for giving me the challenges and the wisdom to realise that it is definitely not "all about me" and that learning to have a servant heart in this world is one of the best ways to exist on this planet. Every day is an opportunity to serve and grow.

Improvement Starts With I.

Thank you.

Tom Hughes

INTRODUCTION

My name is Tom Hughes, and I wrote this book to help people understand what lies at the heart of any great lean transformation.

My objective is to provide a prescriptive, step-by-step manual that solves the problem of people and organisations that want to get started on that journey but simply don't know how.

So, let's start with the big, fundamental question:

What exactly is lean?

This might seem like a very obvious question, but I'm asking it because more than 98% of people who think they have the answer get it wrong.

I say that because, while there are certainly hundreds of companies around the world that successfully "**do lean**," there are thousands more who completely miss the point. They have tried and failed, or even worse, fool themselves into believing they are authentic, **lean** companies, when in fact, what they really have are limp, boring, and wholly uninspiring cultures. If the atmosphere is like that, then it is just not **lean.**

So, I have written this book to help you avoid the **potholes that so many companies have fallen into.**

I feel qualified to write this book because I have decades of experience of transformational change within organisations all over the world, initially not using **lean** as the vehicle but just making change happen the old-fashioned way, with a huge amount of effort and a lot of mistakes. We managed to get some great results, but there was also a lot of collateral damage along the way that tends to accompany such an approach.

Today, I have developed an understanding that makes me see lean as THE best vehicle to take your company wherever you want it to go.

However, I did not always look at lean in this way because I shared the same basic misunderstanding that 98% of people have.

Let me explain.

The opening decade of my career was spent in the automotive supply chain, working directly with Toyota, Nissan, and Honda, among other car manufacturers, practising these advanced manufacturing techniques every day. It wasn't even called "lean" back then (I'm showing my age!), it was just the "Toyota Production System" or doing things the "Japanese way".

I worked at huge first-tier automotive suppliers. My first job was with Rockwell Automotive, a spell in tier 2 plastics at a 100 people firm, then back in tier 1 working in Germany with BTR Automotive.

I worked directly with the source, as most people would agree that modern lean originates from Toyota, so you'd certainly be forgiven for thinking that I really should have known what lean is.

After automotive, I worked for the French multi-national Alstom as a Sourcing Engineering Director for a $400m division before doing an MBA and spending ten years transforming the legendary hydraulic manufacturer Olaer in France and around the world. Five years in supply chain and five years as commercial director. We took that business to $200m before exiting to Parker Hannifin. During this non-automotive spell, I still applied the lean tools and techniques in those businesses. It was a big part of my value added.

When you look at all that, most people would say I'd done some pretty big stuff and that I really had no excuse not to know what lean is.

The truth is that, despite all my experience working with Japanese car manufacturers and all that international, high-level business experience, that I did not.

Until a few years ago, my view of lean would have simply been the textbook answer most people practising lean would give: **"lean is the elimination of waste through continuous improvement"**.

Sounds exciting, doesn't it?

My personal view used to be that lean was an extremely useful set of "tools" – it was super-effective, but as we would say in Ireland, "not much Craic", as in 'not much 'fun'". The misunderstanding I had is very common: lean is done **to** people rather than **with** them. The fundamental problem is that most leaders view lean as being primarily about "process improvement", when in fact, this is not true. Process improvement is just one of the by-products.

When I came on board to spearhead a company transformation in Northern Ireland, where I currently live, I started to correct the error in my thinking. I thought I was joining this company's team to make a strategic shift, to find new markets for their manufacturing technology. Their traditional product market was in sharp decline, so I thought the number one priority would be to win new customers in new segments.

A "Captain of Industry" posture at my
first 2 second lean company

Instead, on day one, the company directors presented me with THEIR top priority. I'll never forget it. Here I was at my new desk, and the two sisters, who were the company's main owners, came up to me and said, "We want you to implement lean".

When I present this story to an audience, I use a picture of Edward Munch's famous painting "The Scream", accompanied by the loud noise of someone screaming painfully, as if from some slasher horror movie. This sums up my reaction: I was horrified.

I hadn't held a shop-floor manufacturing-based role in over ten years, and I thought I was way "past" doing lean. I was much too senior for that!

Me contemplating having to "implement lean"

After getting over my initial shock, my next reaction was, "**where is my team?**" Traditionally, I would have needed at least one person to help collate the key performance measures, facilitate the kaizen workshops, carry out the 5S training and audits, and more. I knew these guys didn't have the budget for that. So, I thought I would reach out to a local government agency – Invest Northern Ireland – as they might be able to provide some funding support, which would at least help me gather the resources I felt necessary to get this thing moving.

So, a couple of weeks later, these guys turned up; they were nice people, initially offering advice about how we could make efficiency improvements and better manage our inventory. I was still not very excited. Then one of the guys, Geoff Crawford, came out with the now immortal line of **"There's this company in Limavady...."** They were World Class at lean, he maintained, a bit like a cult, doing stretches together every morning much as the Japanese do and with extremely high energy, albeit a bit weird. He showed me a YouTube video of this guy called Paul Akers touring their facility. Visually, it blew me away, it really did, but the sheer energy I witnessed that day blew me away even more!!! Just scan the QR code on the picture to watch the video.

Paul Akers: "Seating Matters: Amazing Lean Organisation" https://youtu.be/QwN9g9eO90w

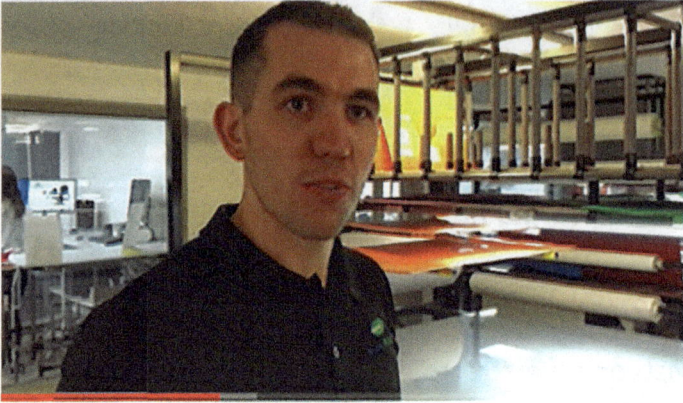

Seating Matters | Amazing Lean Organization

Paul Akers

You will find these pictures with QR codes right the way through the book. Sometimes they take you to a website, but most of the time to a YouTube video that's referred to in the text. If a picture says a thousand words, a video says a million, so I really recommend that you check them out as you come across them. They add immeasurably to the Improvement Starts With I experience!

Anyhow, back to the story...I was fortunate enough that Geoff gave me the number of Ryan Tierney, one of the directors of Seating Matters, who was beyond helpful when I reached out to him on WhatsApp. Ryan said I needed to read a book called *2 Second Lean*, written by Paul Akers – the guy in the YouTube video I had already seen. He also told me Paul himself was very open and easy to communicate with. He recommended I reach out to him directly. I thought this was highly unusual; this guy is a famous author, and I can just drop him a WhatsApp message and he'll get back to me? It seemed a peculiar prospect.

My friend, Ryan Tierney, of Seating Matters, visiting us

Anyhow, I didn't do that at first.

To begin with, I downloaded the audiobook on Audible and listened to it on my way home that night. I had a one-and-a-half-hour commute, so by the time I got home the following evening, I'd listened to the whole thing, as the book is less than four and a half hours long.

The Lean Play App (actually, you can listen to all of Paul's books, including *2 Second Lean* for free on this mobile app that my software company, 3rd Digital, built) https://paulakers.net/lean-play

2 Second Lean Play

Lean Audio Books by Paul Akers

Watch intro video ⓘ

Available on the **App Store**

ANDROID APP ON **Google play**

I will give credit to myself for once: I got a lot of the book's thrust during that first listen. I've listened to it more than a dozen times since, and I liken it to good scripture: each time you visit it, you get something new at another level.

The revelation for me was this: instead of me and maybe a right-hand "champion of lean" type person, along with a few select others in the organisation, "doing lean", 2 Second Lean was a completely different approach. It has a simple structure of having a Morning Meeting every day for the whole company, where everyone learns to see waste and then have time to 3S (Sweep, Sort, and Standardise) and make improvements, applying the learning to their work. No, not some group of smart and elite leaders trying to push the lean train – t**he ENTIRE ORGANISATION does lean.**

So, much easier than the traditional, sporadic approach that was nigh on impossible to sustain. To do this every day? Obvious, at least to me...

The other great news for me personally was that this whole approach really fitted well with my skill set and what I like to do professionally.

I love leadership. I have always loved working with my team, challenging them, supporting them, and ultimately watching them grow. It's one of my all-time favourite career things to do. That's fundamentally what REAL lean is all about. So, instead of being some dry, boring process full of analytics and graphs, sporadic workshops, and consultants, this was all about leadership and engagement at all levels within an organisation.

I was loving this already and really getting excited.

A few weeks after encountering the *2 Second Lean* book, I visited Seating Matters for the first time to have a lean tour. After their amazing Morning Meeting, I spoke to Ryan, and like the good, accomplished, corporate seagull I'd often been up until that point, I asked him, "Hey, Ryan, what are your KPIs [Key Performance Indicators]?" He looked at me strangely and said, "Aw, we don't worry about that. We just focus on growing and developing our people, and we find that the rest just comes..." Luckily, this exchange was caught on video, and the look on my face was hilarious. It was the look of a penny dropping.

Ryan Tierney: "The Look On My Face"
https://youtu.be/hD2Rv7AK5cw

GT Ryan T giving us the essence of Lean

Tom Hughes Lumen GembaDocs Lean

I learnt so much during that day with Ryan and the rest of their outstanding team.

Ryan explained to me that, to begin with, they had wasted 18 months of hard work before even he realised that 2 Second Lean was all about building culture. Like so much in the "lean community", that learning occurred when he visited another world-class lean company in Germany – Michael Althoff's Yellotools. Michael helped him understand that it was all about growing people first, not process improvement. He even pointed out that it says that on the cover of the *2 Second Lean* book. The tagline under the title says, "How to grow people and build a fun lean culture," but 9 out of 10 people miss that...

Most companies approach lean by throwing tools at people without building the culture first and then wonder why it's difficult to keep things going. There's nothing for the tools to hang onto because the people aren't engaged without building culture.

So, let's look at what the word "culture" means.

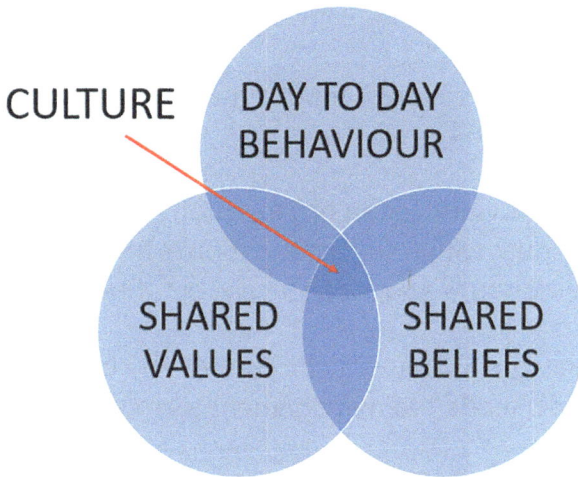

Culture can either be "built" deliberately and nurtured
or be an "accident" because the leaders aren't conscious
of what behaviours, beliefs, and values they reinforce
every day. In my experience, with most non-lean companies,
it's the latter. Even if the company does all the corporate
communication of what they want the culture to be in terms of
posters of visions and values, wall charts, and proclamations,
rarely does the reality of what happens on the ground match
the nice wallpaper. Telling them once and sticking it on the
notice board doesn't work.

This is also the reason for the title of this book – because culture
isn't something "told" to people. Culture cannot be faked, and
every organisation has one.

Culture is living and breathing, and it starts with how the leaders
live and breathe – in actuality. Not how they would like to live
and breathe or behave, but how they actually do it. When the
behaviour, beliefs, and values that are actually practised differ

from those on the wall, then we have a misalignment, and it's not those on the wall that prevail; it's how we do things every day that is real.

So, for all organisations, improvement starts with I because culture starts with I.

While this is obvious for an organisation's leaders, it is true for every individual within an organisation – from the CEO to the new starter. Culture ends collectively, but it begins with you.

When I first got in touch with Paul Akers, my question was, "how do I persuade the management team to do this?"

The answer surprised me, "start with yourself. Start attacking your own waste. You have enough waste for 10 lifetimes. Start with yourself and you will pull the rest with you. Lean is a pull system. Pull not push. You will never push anyone into doing this."

I wasn't the number 1 person at this company, so I couldn't TELL them what to do (not that I would advise that in any case!) so I started on the pull not push strategy.

I started to make improvements in my own work area. I started to make cheesy little improvement videos. I started a WhatsApp group for myself and the rest of the management team to share improvements. I encouraged the rest of the management team to read / listen to the book. I started talking about waste in all my standup meetings. I started to get people curious about what this was all about.

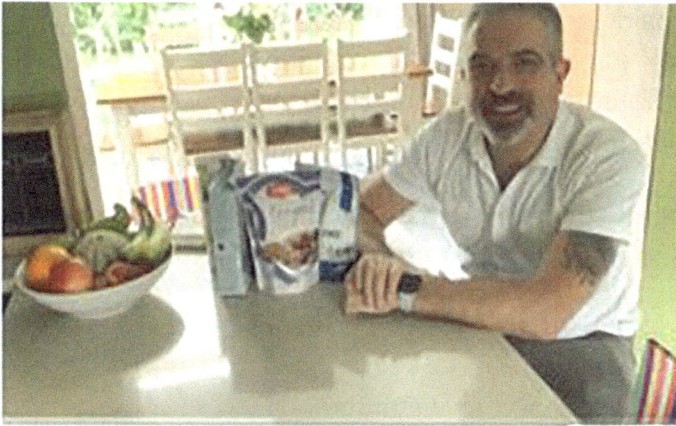

Tom Morning Smoothie Improvement

Tom Hughes Lumen GembaDocs Lean

Starting with I, I became an overnight Lean Maniac.

I was not the company owner but even if I had been, this is the right approach. "You will never push into anyone into doing Lean."

Whether you're the company owner or the new starter who just got bitten by the Lean bug. Improvement starts with I. It's a pull system! You lead by example and become a magnet for the rest. It might not happen overnight, it takes time and perseverance but it is also the most fun and fulfilling journey you will ever take in your career once you get momentum.

Again, a lean culture is something special, and it's a good idea to clarify where the journey may start for most organisations and the difference we are aiming for when growing people to build a lean culture together.

This is HUGE because many of your team members may never have been asked, "How can we do this better?" Regardless of the slogans mounted on the wall, many may reckon they have been paid just for the work of their hands. They have been there to "just do their job", punch the clock – whether in reality or just figuratively – and are not asked to use their heads much by doing a lot of thinking.

It's great to clarify what we mean when we say we are growing people and building a lean culture together.

It means we are ALL going to:

Learn to think and behave differently

Learn to see waste

Learn to leave our egos at the door

Learn to collaborate as equals

Learn to act creatively and run experiments to make improvements

Learn to embrace failure in the pursuit of excellence

Learn to bring mistakes to the surface, not hide them

Learn to speak without offending and listen without defending

Learn to have fun getting better at what we do every day

Build strong, cohesive bonds in our entire team

Take pride in becoming the best in the world at what we do

This is what "growing and developing people" means. That's the bar. It's about stimulating each of us to "want" to do this and learning to be "able" to do this.

Some of us will "get it" straight away. Others will take longer. Others still might be repelled by it and never get it. Led properly, though, that number will be few, as the vast majority of people would much rather come to a workplace where they are truly valued, respected, and encouraged to grow.

I would argue that the prevailing attitude in the world today is, "Everyone wants everyone else to change to make the world suit them". It's a lazy, passive attitude and one that means you as an individual are disempowering yourself because you're in control of nothing; everyone else is "doing it".

Improvement starts with I means that, when there's a problem, you look at what you can do about it, how you can contribute, and what you can change. This goes from the top to the bottom of the organisation chart.

I have lost count of the number of times I've interacted with a leader, manager, or team member who says, "Why won't 'they' do X?" and "Why aren't 'they' doing X?" When I ask, "Well, are you doing it?" the answer is always – and I mean *always* – the same: "no", along with some mumbled phrase like, "I hadn't thought of it like that..."

You can't sell what you haven't bought yourself. Be the behaviour you want to see.

The simple structure and discipline of a morning meeting builds culture and solves this problem when executed with purpose. This is because expectations are set and behaviour is reinforced as a team with every single person, every single day. No ambiguity. It is beautiful in its simplicity.

It was only a week or two after my first visit to Seating Matters that I started on my own lean journey with that first company and began to really apply this principle.

Since then, I've been extremely fortunate to have had the opportunity to lead or help other people get started on theirs. This has led me to develop an overall process to create the environment and make the most of that system every time. It works to drive engagement, improvement, and results in a variety of environments. In that order. Hands (everyone's doing that, lean or not), then hearts, then heads!

This is a really important point to make this early on; that is the order of proceedings.

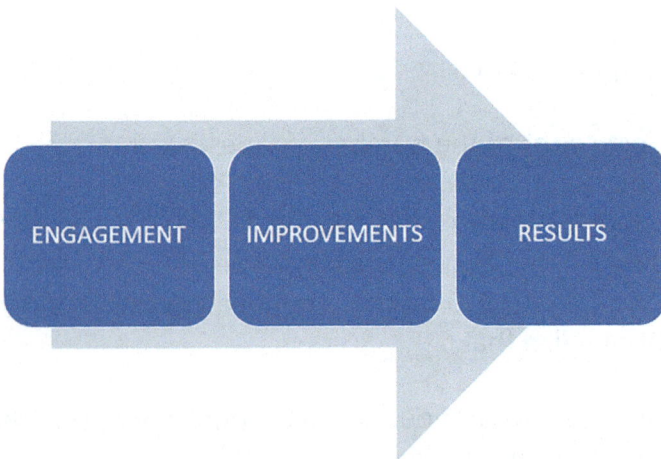

That is the process, and it's simple.

If you can pick up a broom, you can be engaged – we all can. And to be successful, we all MUST – from the CEO to the junior starter, from the office people to the operational staff. No exceptions.

This levels the playing field, building mutual respect for everyone, regardless of their place on the organisation chart. Everyone realises that they matter.

If everyone starts to raise standards by cleaning the work environment every day, they will soon begin to ask questions like:

- Do we have enough brooms?
- Management, can we buy more brooms – yes/no? Will management support us?
- Why do I struggle to find the brooms every day?
- We need a place for each broom... Maybe we should standardise where they are kept?
- Where is all this dirt coming from?
- Can we fix it at the source?
- Why is X broken?
- Why do we have so many?

And on and on and on. As we develop, we find more problems when we clean. We ask more and more questions and providing that leadership support appropriately, that foundation of engagement is layered with knowledge, we see improvements, and as we become more productive through countless Improvements, we get results.

Too many people fail because they want results straight away, or even improvements. It simply doesn't work that way. Lean is built on hearts. It is built on engagement. Like Ryan Tierney says, if you get that, "the rest just comes".

As we say in lean, "Everything in life is a process or the outcome of a process", and the process we present in this book adds even more clarity to the contents of Paul's book, acting as a set of stabilisers that can help you avoid some of the pitfalls if you "just do it". So, I strongly advise you to read and digest Paul's book as well as diving into this one.

Our process consists of the "Five Cs":

Candour
Commitment
Coaching
Consistency
Continuous Learning

These are the key steps you need to go through in order to REALLY do lean. If any of them are missed, you WILL fail. It's like a bird trying to fly on a broken wing: you and your organisation will flap around a lot, but your efforts will not get off the ground!

All of them require effort from the individual and collective energy from the organisation, but when you put in that energy to build the new culture, the energy required to sustain it will be less. It's like building a new habit or quitting an old one: it can be tough at the beginning, but it gets easier.

Improvement Starts With I can help your organisation become a shining beacon of success, making your life easier, more fun, and without the normal daily friction and fire-fighting.

It's a simple process but not easy. Like Michael Althoff says, "Lean is hard work that makes life easy".

I often use the imagery with entire client organisations of people driving to work with their fingers tapping on the steering wheel. Is that you right now? Would you like it to be?

Well, read on!

PS: at the end of each chapter, I list the key TAKEAWAYS for that given chapter.

I hope you find them useful.

Enjoy!

- Most people misunderstand lean as being primarily about improving processes when it is really about building culture and growing people, and that starts with each of us as individuals – "I".

- Lean is not a dry, analytical process; it is a vehicle to drive complete team engagement and total participation.

- Lean needs to be reinforced every day, or it will always be very difficult to build or sustain a real lean culture.

CHAPTER 1

The First "C" – CANDOUR

The Oxford English Dictionary defines "Candour" as: **"The quality of being open and honest; frankness".**

Let's get this out of the way quickly: Candour is the foundation upon which any great lean organisation is built.

You could justifiably say that no one gets to live a truly outstanding life without a strong dose of directness. It's about being able to be honest with yourself and others so that changes can be triggered. Without Candour, things become stuck.

Rather unfortunately, though, Candour has become an increasingly rare commodity in today's society. From our education systems breeding a culture of awarding everyone a medal to parents only wanting to "be positive" with their children, it has led to a situation where real Candour can be considered shocking. That conditioning over recent decades has led to the common belief that **"nice is good" and "directness is rude".** Quite frankly, it's a shame!

The result of this inability to be honest with oneself and with other people leads to a huge amount of dysfunction in our lives. I'm not just talking about the workplace but also in our personal lives. "Niceness" is often another word for just being too weak to express one's dissatisfaction, and this form of niceness is certainly not the altruistic act it is often portrayed to be.

The thing is, making that choice to be nice but weak or direct and candid is a personal one, and that's why we can say that Candour starts with I.

Often, people take the "nice" option because it is easy in the short term. However, being too nice is often the root cause of why most companies have internal dysfunctions between owners, individuals, and departments. People don't have the courage to tackle situations head-on and instead walk out of meetings with the important things left unsaid, only for the bitching to happen behind closed doors and among friendly colleagues. Meanwhile, the walls of the silos only grow higher, and the dysfunction grows worse, all while the organisational environment becomes stagnant and stale. In the long term, a lack of Candour costs big.

My good friend Alex Ramirez (a 25-year oil and gas veteran of senior positions and who was responsible for probably the best lean culture implementation in the world during 2020. I kid you not!) told me a great story about how Candour had impacted his lean journey. He told me it was the MAIN REASON they got started down this road.

Here is his story.

"I used to go to one of our plants every month to review their progress with our continuous improvement team methodology that we as an entire company had been following for 20 years". (This is a multi-billion-dollar organisation!). "It was a tedious, systematic, tool-driven approach that had our guys presenting data to discuss problems, which sounds good, but there is a lot of waste there. We were focused more on using tools and presenting graphs on a nice little dashboard than actually having people just fix what bugs them. We had a recently new plant manager, a great guy, and I asked him, "Why is this **** not working?" Why is it every time I come that we go over this same stuff, and it's not working?' And he looked back at me and asked, 'Alex, do you really want to know the truth?' 'Of course, dude, WTF?' Then he replied, 'We're just putting on a show for you to be happy. That's the truth. This **** doesn't work'.

I replied, 'Thanks so much. Let me get back to you on that'.

Then I thought about it and thought about it, and I was like, how could I miss this? Like, how could I not see that they were just doing it to please me? And I'm just expecting this formula to work.

Then Edson showed me 2 Second Lean, and I was like, 'This is it! This is it!' and I contacted Paul (Akers) and the rest is history.

However, it was that candid moment when my team could tell me to my face that 'we are just ****ing pleasing you. This stuff doesn't work. It's just more of the same'.

I had a big hansei (self-reflection) to myself, and what I found was that what I was offering these guys was not worthy, and it's hard because that was the corporate norm; you apply the continuous improvement team methodology, and you expect to have the results. It's just following the book. I was being a good student but then having to take that decision and having to go against the establishment, that this stuff that's been around 20 years but I've learnt is not good.

I needed to find something better for these guys.

When I showed 2 Second Lean to that original Plant Manager and he started running with it, he saw great results, but when I started to do it in Houston, and I was there every morning, the results were just amazing."

This story shows the four stages of Candour necessary to have a truly great lean culture. Those four stages are:

- The courage to STOP
- The courage to SPEAK UP
- The courage to LISTEN
- The courage to ACT

For lean to flourish and Candour to become a part of the culture, we need to foster all four of these aspects. A lot of what needs to be done is to eliminate any fear in the organisation so that people feel safe enough to exhibit this kind of behaviour.

To get started, someone needs to have the cojones to "pull the andon" (the Japanese have a stop cord that anyone on the line can pull when there's a problem, and production stops until they fix it – a perfect example of "Raising Defects"). If that facility is not there, then things generally just carry on being dysfunctional and stale.

In Alex's case, he was motivated to take **the first step to STOP** just by being fed up with going through the motions. Essentially, he was just "fixing what bugs him"! If he hadn't stopped, the rest of the process might never have happened. They could still be having their boring, not very effective CIT meetings, and their lean journey would never have gotten off the ground!

For 20 odd years, the management team of that plant (and the entire organisation, for that matter) had presented their graphs to the seagull coming from corporate (that's Alex in this case!), and everyone just kept on repeating the process without questioning it. The chances are that everyone involved found the process tedious, even hating it, but they all kept up the charade with no one ever stopping to ask, "Does this make any sense?"

The thing is, SOMEONE has to have that courage to call BS, and that's where *Improvement Starts With I* comes in. There's no good waiting for someone else to do it: YOU have to do it when there is a struggle or a mindless, wasteful routine that becomes evident.

For leaders in an organisation, *Improvement Starts With I* because you need to lead by example by calling STOP when it becomes evident that a process is working below par. A big part of a lean leader's role is to make it safe for their team members to STOP, too, creating what is known in lean circles as a STOP culture. This needs to be incorporated into your behaviour. We will go through that in the next steps.

The second step, "**SPEAK UP**", would be Candour in its most traditional form, the meaning that most people think of when they hear the word. That is both Alex and the Plant Manager having the courage **to SPEAK UP** and discuss openly why the sacred corporate cow was not working.

How often have we witnessed the STOP moment, especially when the big boss stops and there is a stony silence as we just carry on with business as usual? No one is brave enough to take the chance and speak up to say what is needed.

Speaking Up is a function of courage and safety. The courage part is on the individual, and the safety part is the job of leadership to create that safe environment where problems are surfaced, not hidden, and processes, not people, are attacked.

In Alex's instance, it's important he wasn't SPEAKING UP to point out someone else's failure or accuse them of anything. He was stopping to ask **why is this process not working?** He wasn't blaming anyone or attacking them; he was bugged by the process, not the people, which is a big distinction, and he was taking responsibility for the situation with his Candour in stopping. Improvement starts with I.

A common problem for business leaders is to look at their organisation's culture, processes, and systems and wonder why they're not as good as they would like them to be. Often, the leader's first reaction will be to blame influences other than themselves – for example, "It's hard to get good people today", "People don't want to work in our area", "We can't get people," "Corporate say we have to do it this way", etcetera, etcetera.

This attitude is usually the prevailing one regarding the majority of business leaders. They will not accept responsibility for the situation they find themselves in, which means they feel powerless to influence it, which means they do not take action to change.

This is an illustration of "Improvement Starts with I". In this case, where it doesn't start at all.

I'm here to tell you that this attitude is **total nonsense**.

There are world-class companies everywhere with great people who are completely engaged and produce outstanding work in the same environment in which your company has become dysfunctional. Seating Matters literally have waiting lists of people wanting to work there, and to get in the door is not easy. Yet, practically every other company in our area really struggles to get a warm, upright body to work for them.

What's the difference? I hear you ask. Simple: it's **leadership**.

The truth is that, no matter what company culture looks like – good or not so good – **you as the leader created it,** no one else – not the government, not society at large, and certainly not some conjecture that people aren't as good as they used to be. You hired the people, even if you didn't directly; therefore, it's your responsibility. Your behaviour sets the tone. What you tolerate, you accept. Unfortunately, what is true in most organisations that don't have a lean culture is that they have simply become comfortable with their dysfunction. They believe the dysfunction is "normal" and just something that needs to be tolerated. The outliers and the world-class companies among us prove that this is not the case.

Even if you aren't one of the business leaders in your organisation, whatever position you happen to occupy, you are there now – no one else put you there. Spiritually, you are exactly where you are supposed to be. It's karma, baby, karma. There are no accidents.

The great news about this simple truth is that **when you do it, you can undo it**. You are in control of what happens next. You are in control of building something better. The thing is, though, as Einstein famously said, "A problem cannot be solved at the same level of consciousness as that on which it was created". So you need to raise your level or get out of the way and let someone else do it.

Taking that level of responsibility for your situation is not easy for many people, but if you can manage to do it, it is a liberating experience for most. It can be quite stressful trying to control other people, as well as any external factors that may arise. When you take this level of responsibility and the realisation that you did it, then your first job is to assess yourself and your own contribution to the current status quo and work on that.

This can really get deep, and some fundamental questions call for real Candour. You need to ask yourself about how you see not only the world but **your own attitudes and beliefs** that will determine whether you have what it takes to be a real lean leader.

For leaders, it's about **believing that people are fundamentally good and actually want to do a good job**. We can see that Alex had this deeply held belief even before he consciously started on his real lean journey.

If your belief system includes thinking that people are just not built that way and will do as little as they can get away with and can't be trusted, then it's going to be extremely difficult for you to be a leader within a lean organisation.

Lean leaders "come out of the box" with **a deep caring and respect for other people**. If that isn't an already embedded character trait of yours, then it's very hard to learn and impossible to fake. Essentially, to have that, you need to have humility towards others in a certain way, which means that you don't actually believe you have all the answers; your entire team can contribute towards creating a better company.

Lean leaders think their team has all the answers. Managers (those who are not lean leaders but occupy a supervisory position on the organisational chart!) think that they themselves have all the answers and that the team just needs to be told what to do. If you're in the latter camp, you need to change this attitude or start polishing your resume if your company is serious about leading a lean future.

We recently discussed this in the Lean Maniacs group (a chat group on Signal founded by Dave Lelonek of Sticky RX for Lean people to share best practise and improvements – it's amazing!) on the difference between the 3 types of leadership: "Dictators" who just tell people to "do it my way", "Empowerment types" who just tell people to "do it your way" with little or no guidance, and finally, "Lean Style" who say "follow me, and we will figure this out together".

This latter style is what we are after!

In this way, lean leaders aren't telling but are much more about "asking". Not giving prescriptive solutions to the team but helping them solve problems creatively, never relinquishing ownership for the challenges. When leaders give people answers to their problems, in a way, they also take responsibility for solving them, which is not a good thing for anyone involved. No one grows in this scenario.

I had some early training on this in my second automotive job, when I was a young Quality Manager. Every morning, I would do my rounds of the plastic injection moulding shop, around 40 different machines and production areas. This led to me wanting to know about any ongoing problems that my nature immediately made me want to fix for my colleagues. Not because I was a dictator but simply because I was a good-natured chap who didn't know any better. Thankfully, my Operations Director above me could see what was happening.

By the time I'd finished my round, I'd get back to my desk, heavily weighted down after having collected at least half a dozen problems that I had personally taken on the responsibility for solving.

He said to me, "Do you know that you've just picked up a bunch of monkeys?"

I replied that I had no clue what he was talking about.

He described the process of me engaging with one of the tool setters on problems with a setup.

He said, "He has a problem, a monkey, and he wants to give it away to someone. He sees you coming, and he's very happy to let you have it. For that monkey to be put on your back!"

When he explained the scenario this way, the penny dropped!

His advice was to help, coach, support, and ask questions but never to accept the monkey. Keep it where it belongs!

It was great advice that has never left me. **Keep the monkeys where they belong.** It's better for everyone.

For lean to work properly, it must be authentic. It must be about building culture and growing people at its heart. Have that as your genuine focus, and the results will come.

Again, back to the beginning of my career. At Rockwell, all of us who worked there wore the same green uniform – from junior engineers like me to the operators on the shop floor and right up to senior managers.

There weren't any "management" car parking spaces or a "management" canteen; we all used the same car park and the same eating area. There was a visitors' bathroom at reception, but apart from that, we all used the same set of bathrooms.

Our culture was heavily influenced by our main customers, who happened to be Japanese auto manufacturers.

I worked as a quality engineer, and when we responded to quality concerns, our customers would not let us write "operator error" on the corrective action documents. This would have been traditional up until that point. All the European customers, such as GM, were much more laid back about such things. It was drilled into us by our Japanese customers that it was ALWAYS a process issue, never a people issue. If someone made a mistake, it was because the process was not robust or clear enough or the operator had not been adequately trained. There always had to be a real root cause, a process, or a system issue. We could not just blame the individual.

So, I had these beliefs and attitudes engrained into me within this environment, and therefore I felt that I already "got lean" at this level. If you're reading this and these points resonate, brilliant! If that doesn't sound like the kind of environment you would enjoy, it could be a time to reflect.

Coming back to our Alex example, the original Plant Manager trusted him because he already knew that Alex walked and talked these values, so it felt safe for him to speak up.

If you want to have real Candour within your organisation, it's especially important for the leaders to start thinking and acting in this way. **Make it safe for the people yet attack bad processes every day.**

As for the rest of the organisation, be brave! When you see a problem that is in YOUR area, within YOUR scope of control, SPEAK UP and get on with the process of addressing it.

The third essential component of Candour is the courage to listen and introspect.

When we listen to Alex's story, he received information that, on the one hand, he asked for, but on the other – and this is important – is a problem that he would rather not be hearing!

This is a component of Candour that is rarely talked about. Everyone focuses on giving out feedback, but what good is that if we don't have an environment where that Candour can be respectfully received?

We had an expression that my leadership mentor at Olaer (an amazing gentleman called Angus McLeod) drilled into us. It was actually one of the ground rules that we would re-iterate at the beginning of our international meetings:

"SPEAK WITHOUT OFFENDING. LISTEN WITHOUT DEFENDING."

It would have been so easy for Alex to go into self-defence mode of fight or flight when the Plant Manager told him about the corporate wallpaper they had been putting up for so long. It can seem like a personal attack when someone points out a failing in what you've been doing or how you've been behaving, which is why even when we are giving Candour, we should be careful to be as respectful around the language we use as we possibly can be, especially when a situation is heated. It is something that requires self-control.

In Alex's case, he felt foolish. He had been part of this charade for years. "How could I have missed this?"

In my experience, it takes a deeply secure person to be able to receive Candour in this way.

Insecure people tend to puff out their chests and go on the offensive or try to deflect the problem. Of course, if our environment is like that, who's going to exhibit Candour? Only the very brave or the very stupid...

Secure people have the maturity to be bigger than their instinctive drive to go into fight or flight. They can take a deep breath, relax, and ask for more dialogue. Instead of trying to run away or defend, they can "lean in" and ask for more to get to the "why?"

That type of behaviour might not be natural for everyone, but with practise, the response can become habitual. We need to build a culture that both drives out fear and makes it safe for people to surface problems. To build Candour, it's SAFETY FIRST!

The fourth essential aspect of Candour is to ACT.

Angus also used to use another quote: "Vision without action is a daydream. Action without vision is a nightmare". I've since found out that it is commonly claimed to be a "Japanese proverb" or has sometimes been attributed to Soichiro Honda.

At the end of the day, we can have all the stopping, speaking up, and listening, but if it is not followed up by action, wasn't it all just hot air?

Alex realised that he had to offer "something else", and when he was presented 2 Second Lean by Edson, here was the solution to take into action. By doing so, he finally allowed the innate energy of the organisation to express itself.

If we take a step back to reflect, I'm sure that everyone reading this who has ever worked in an organisation of more than two people can relate to this simple four step Candour process!

An easy one to pick is that meeting we all hate but we all just go along with it, go through the motions, and no one speaks up!

My own personal worst example of this was when I worked at Olaer and our CEO insisted on bringing together around 20 of the most senior people in the company, most of them Managing Directors of entire countries, for two days every single month. It was the worst organised meeting structure I've ever witnessed.

Typically, the agenda tried to do far too much. Everyone's presentation overran its timing. Then we would try to make decisions on strategic issues. That was the worst part. Trying to make a decision with 20-odd strong-willed people was like pulling teeth. I likened those discussions to making the decision to operate on someone, opening them up, poking around for a few hours, and then just leaving them, wound wide open. It would have been better all-round if we'd never bothered in the first place, as all we did was create a lot of damage in terms of arguments and bruised egos without having resolved anything.

It was also common practice for people to sit answering emails on their laptops while someone presented to the group, which I found desperately rude.

The meetings started at 8.30 in the morning and rarely finished before 7.30 at night. It was exhausting. They were the only times that I genuinely thought about resigning from the company I dearly loved, and that is the absolute truth.

Eventually, I'd just had enough: I pulled the **stop** cord. I cornered my CEO, (now a good friend called Mike Blenkinsop) and had the courage to **speak up**. I told him that I thought that the meetings were ****. (Hardly speak without offending, but I don't pretend to be perfect!). I told him about the worst issues and asked if I could have the opportunity to run it my way. He found it unsettling, but to his credit, he **listen**ed anyway. In the end, he was happy to agree because he hated running them too. So, in the end, it was not that difficult to **act**.

It's amazing how it often takes just one single person to exhibit Candour about a bad situation, and then everyone heaves a sigh of relief that someone has finally broken the cycle! It wasn't "my job" to take responsibility for fixing this problem, but that's what lean people do. It doesn't matter where we sit in the organisational chart – we step up and **take total responsibility.**

I ran those meetings like Genghis Tom. Total clarity. Total Candour.

Every meeting started with the ground rules: speak without offending, listen without defending. No open laptops or answering emails during the meeting – every presenter would have the full and respectful attention of all present. Half-hour breaks were planned, allowing people to socialise and attend to urgent operational issues.

We had strict agendas and timings. Everyone who presented had to send me their presentations at least three days before the meeting, and I would vet them for quality and quantity of content – no more 80 slide presentations for a half-hour slot.

I designed the meeting to be predominantly about one-way communication. One person to many. No big discussions. Anything that needed a decision, I asked for a show of hands of people who cared passionately about subject X, and they could form a working group that would present back to the entire group on their decision at the next meeting. No more endless open heart surgery discussions.

We finished and started on time, so people could chat informally, socialise, and build connections – which was the real reason for the meeting in the first place.

It was just a black and white transformation, and everyone – and I mean everyone – just loved it.

We all really looked forward to the meetings, so fun and productive and having the time to build friendships.

It takes just one person to exhibit Candour, and that pent-up, frustrated energy can be released. That one person can be anyone. **Improvement Starts With I.**

I recently discussed this kind of Candour with one of my lean buddies, Brannon Burton of Sunrok Construction, and he told me about a practice he does with new recruits that blew me away.

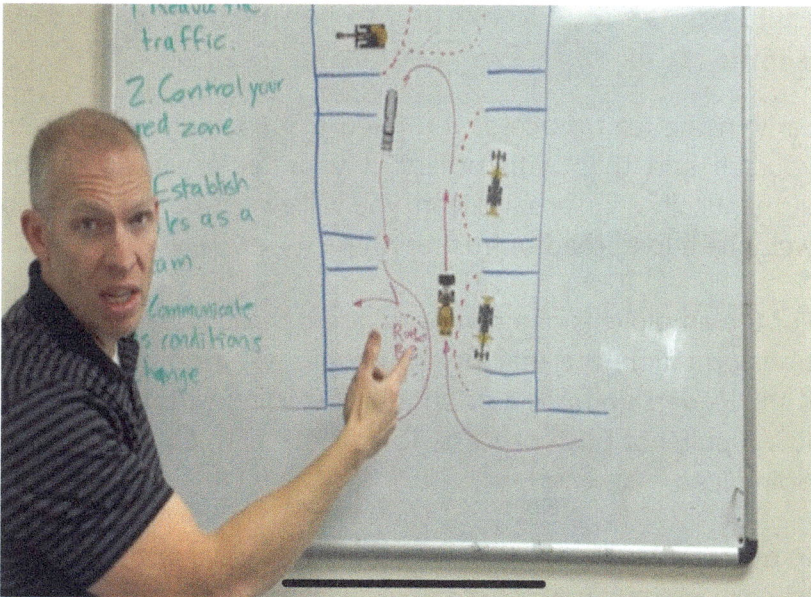

Brannon explaining waste in one of our Lean Maniac videos

He said that when he is bringing someone new on board, he tells them he sometimes may tell them things they don't want to hear – not because he wants to be an a-hole but because he genuinely cares about their success and wants them to have the best feedback. Like many people, he himself finds Candour difficult. Taking this approach allows him to set the groundwork: there is "nothing wrong with you".

This means they will know early on if there are course corrections they need to make. The really important message here is that it's not about the person delivering the feedback – the energy behind it is a giving energy; it's there to help the person receiving it.

He sets the individual's expectations to expect Candour and gives them an opportunity to understand the intention behind it. Now that's leadership!

Building Candour – change the people or change the people

Early in the lean process, you need to be candid – first with yourself and then with others. If your team will not 100% authentically align around lean, you will always be pulling dead weight – a long road of frustration.

For the employees of a company going through a lean culture transformation, the majority of people will absolutely join in if the leadership does a good job of starting with themselves. It is a pull, not push process. You will never push anyone into doing lean.

In my experience, with creating change in organisations, there will always be early adopters who "get it" straight away and want to run with the change. Great! Encourage them and give them tons of recognition to pull the people on the fence to come on board.

There will be a bigger group who will want to wait and see. "Are they really serious about this?" We could view them as the "silent majority". When you start having Morning Meetings, you will know what I mean! There can be a variety of reasons for this. It just takes most people time to understand what is happening and buy into it. The leadership needs patience around that. We will delve more into that later in the book.

There are also invariably people who just don't enjoy lean done in this way; they think they are above it. That's the candid truth. "What's all this waste business? I know this already. Why do we have to do this every day?"

They don't open their hearts to it and resist the change in their minds. Often, these people were doing really well in the "old system" of tribal knowledge, where they held power because they were the best firefighters and on some kind of pedestal for it. Playing as equals in the team can be a big dent in their ego, so they resist.

Now, it's not that these people can't be won over with great leadership – they certainly can. However, my advice is to be honest with yourself – be really candid: are you willing to make the hard changes that might be necessary to win a fantastic lean culture? Sometimes, those people will just have to go.

I've personally seen it too often – in a family business, for example, where the "lean guy" is constantly frustrated at the culture not taking hold, without realising it's the lack of alignment in the senior team that his people experience every day which is holding things back. It takes a lot more work to build a culture than it does to tear it down. One ill-placed comment from a non-aligned leader to a staff member ripples through the whole organisation, especially in a small to medium company, and it's clear to all that the company as a whole doesn't really mean it. Frustration and mediocrity will continue without action to resolve the root cause. If, for one reason or another, you can't or more likely don't want to **"change the people or change the people,"** don't try to go down the lean road. Here is some serious Candour from me!

Those individuals can choose for themselves about how they want to respond to Lean, but if they aren't willing or able to change, the choice needs to be made for them. They need to be moved on by Leadership.

I'm not beating around the bush here, and if you're serious about lean, neither will you or your organisation's leadership.

Paul Akers fired his brother-in-law early on in their lean journey because he was actively obstructing progress. I know of other similar examples within the lean community. If you want greatness, you need total Candour and alignment.

In my first 2 Second Lean organisation, there was daily inter-personal friction and sometimes screaming arguments. It was pretty toxic, but I never saw anyone actually get fired, no matter what the problem was. So, when we started with Morning Meetings and preaching "respect for people", it was a huge shift, and the vast majority of people embraced it. Like, why not? However, there is always one! Or maybe two or three.

We had a relatively new team member who wouldn't get on board with lean, especially the 3S and cleaning part integral to building culture. He eventually told his team leader to "**** off!" and tried to intimidate him physically. When I heard about this, I told the senior team that he had to go – no exceptions.

I encountered the "we are struggling to get people" and "he's really good at X" arguments that many reading this would have heard before. I responded that this level of disrespect had to be met with zero tolerance. NO EXCEPTIONS.

None of them wanted to fire this guy. "You do it!" I was told.

Well, *Improvement Starts with I*, so I took responsibility, got on the phone with the guy, and fired him on the spot. With Candour, I told him exactly why. That kind of behaviour would never be tolerated here. He couldn't believe it, as he had bought into the story that no one was ever fired from this place...

The next day in the Morning Meeting, I told the rest of the team that he was gone and why and that things were changing! I'll be best friend to those who want to get on our train and be patient with those still getting used to the idea, but if you're actually against us, I will enjoy firing you. Not because I'm a nasty individual but because I see it as the right thing to do so that the rest of us can have a world-class place to work. Candour like this breeds clarity, and generally, people like that!

The short-term "easy" route would have been just to go with the flow of the senior management team, but Improvement Starts with I – especially when it comes to Candour.

When I worked in France doing a culture turnaround, one of the French senior managers told me this phrase, "*Pour encourager les autres*". It comes from the times of the French revolution and means "to encourage the rest", used in reference to public beheadings by guillotine!

It's simple: if you are a leader, you might have to "*encourager les autres*" if someone is blatantly not getting on board with the change. It shows that leadership is serious about the change and differentiates between those that are coming on board and those that are not. If leadership openly tolerates people fighting with the system, soon, the others will ask themselves, "Why am I bothering?" and stop putting the effort into lean. Don't measure the evolution of your organisation by the behaviour of those at the top end of your lean engagement – measure it by those at the bottom. If you are one of the "*autres*", it's time for you to change or be changed. Either get on board or find somewhere else to pursue your career. There's some more Candour for you.

A common problem is the "we can't do it without X person" phenomenon I mentioned above. Even though this individual behaves like an a-hole and you've had umpteen conversations about it, they don't change. However, they've got so much knowledge or are such a hard worker that the leadership team is worried if they can survive without them.

My own experience and that of countless other lean leaders is that there has to be zero tolerance when it comes to embracing lean, especially for senior people. The only problem is waiting and tolerating a bad apple in the barrel for too long. Just do it.

Especially if it's a manager, you will likely find a wealth of energy and creativity waiting to be unleashed when that person moves on. No one is bigger than the company, and even if there are a few weeks of disruption while you work out how to fill the gap, it is always much better in the medium term.

If you move people out, make sure you apply good screening to anyone you move in. One screening tool we use at Lumen is to get people to read *2 Second Lean* during the recruitment process and then quiz them on it. Either they get it, or they don't, and if they don't get it, we don't let them in.

With time, with your internal lean culture-building process and a filter to only bring great people in, your culture will only get stronger and stronger. **Change the people or change the people.**

Candour and eliminating organisational friction

We have looked at the process of aligning individuals within the team with lean using the change the people or change the people approach, but often there are things beyond the individual and even the department level that will inhibit lean from taking hold within an organisation.

From experience, I have found that, in particular, the organization's key performance indicators, and more specifically any departmental targets, can be a huge cause of fiction, conflict, and internal dysfunction.

I've seen the patterns repeat over and over.

Sales departments are driven purely by sales and engage in friction-creating activities, like making delivery promises they know will likely not be kept by production to win orders and hit targets.

Supply chains are driven by production output, without on-time delivery or quality targets, leading to small individual order lines becoming months late with lots of screaming customers that sales and service people have to deal with.

Purchasing is beaten up for inventory levels, either having too much or too little stock without any ownership from sales for the forecasting they were buying against.

Engineering departments just cover their ass because all they care about is not getting blamed for failures, so everything is over-engineered and too expensive to make and sell.

Those are just a few, and most pre-lean companies will have some obvious inter-departmental conflict that is obvious to the senior leadership team but has just become part of the "normal dysfunction".

Even just the "cadence" that a business mainly runs on causes dysfunction. Most businesses are driven by the month, which causes huge unevenness with production rushes at the month-end, resulting in stress and endless waste. Changing the focus to weekly or daily just smooths things out. I've seen that effect so many times.

My second job in automotive had me as a quality manager of a one-hundred people company. My office was located just at the corner of the shopfloor on the main thoroughfare to the warehouse despatch area. This was where I got to see the KPI/cadence effect first-hand.

Every day was the same rhythm. Everything was relatively calm until about 3.30 pm. Then, up until 5 pm, which was our finish time, pandemonium! People literally ran up the aisle with boxes to be despatched when we got closer to 5 o'clock.

The reason?

Our psychopath Managing Director had a sales target of £25,000 a day. If that was met, great! If that wasn't met, he would come down to the shopfloor in his three-piece suit, turn purple, and make like a hairdryer to the Production Manager, team leaders, and anyone else unfortunate enough to be within shouting distance!

Now, I'm not saying that this is a good thing! It's just that whatever your consequential measure, it will dictate your business's rhythm, which can really create problems.

During my French turnaround, the monthly sales graph was like a hockey stick, and that was just because no one from management really cared about sales until the last week of the month, when they would have to report to their masters, so the rush was always then.

So, for us, just to smooth it out better, we moved to weekly measures. Guess what? No more hockey stick. Simple.

Let's surface those kinds of issues within your organisation now. Be candid with each other as a team and start to have measures that build alignment, not create barriers towards it.

For that to happen, we need Candour within our team, with each of us taking responsibility. Forget the past; it's about getting better. Improvement Starts with I.

As well as the KPIs, simply how people are paid can be a major issue in some organisations. We need to align pay with the behaviour we expect or, as a minimum, make sure that how we pay people is not an active disincentive to teamwork and improvement.

At the first business where I implemented 2 Second Lean, the financial incentives for the shopfloor were one of the biggest problems to moving forward with lean. In fact, I insisted that we didn't even start with Morning Meetings and the rest of the process until we had resolved it.

An ancient piece-rate system was in place, paying people purely on output. If a worker had poor output, he got minimum wage. This led to people specialising in a particular machine, informally becoming "their machine" because they could easily hit the target. They didn't want to cross-train to learn new machines because they would be on a minimum wage during the training period. They also didn't want to waste time training other people because they would then lose output, find themselves on minimum wage, and lose the hold on "their machine".

Let's just say that it didn't encourage teamwork.

An attendance bonus was also in place that the same 80% of people received all the time and the rest never did. If you were late a single morning or missed a day, you lost a month. Most of the time, when someone was late or missed a day, they did it multiple times in the month. It clearly didn't do anything to motivate anyone.

It was a big challenge to convince the leadership team to drop this structure and move to a different one, but we did it. This idea of metrics and payment leading the organisation and not the actual leadership people is not an uncommon situation. They were relying on the payment structure to manage the people and were worried output would fall.

It did not, and taking the time to change the payment structure before we started Morning Meetings worked a treat. It showed the entire organisation that we were very serious about change.

Change payment structure...

NEW PAYMENT STRUCTURE

GRADE	No. of tasks / machines	HANDS						HEART					HEAD				RATE		
WHITE BELT	< 10 tasks / machines																£ 8.82		
GREEN BELT	10 - 20 tasks / machines	X	X	X	X		X	X	X	X	X		X				£ 10.11	10	9
BROWN BELT	10 - 20 tasks / machines	X	X	X	X	X	X	X	X	X	X	X	X	X			£ 11.61	13	12
BLACK BELT	20 + tasks / machines	X	X	X	X	X	X	X	X	X	X	X	X	X	X	X	£ 13.11	15	15

Orange areas are Subject to Management Audit & number of tasks / machines increases to keep those points for next grade

Number of tasks / machines is currently being developed and is subject to change but will always be in the spirit of fairness.

The payment structure we moved to in my first 2 Second Lean company

We changed to a new payment structure based on three main categories: hands, heart, and head. We explained that we had only paid for output historically, but now the hands meant how many different machines they could skilfully operate. Heart was about how well they worked within the team, and head was about how they contributed to improvements and developed their leadership skills. It provided a clear pathway to show everyone how they could progress within the company and laid out very clearly what we wanted from the team members.

The two main business owners and I sat down with every single team member face to face and explained the change, why we were doing it, and that lean was now the only way forward. No exceptions. We took responsibility to communicate the change effectively, eyeball to eyeball with Candour.

Incidentally, we even changed job titles. We moved from "Operators" to "Team Members" and from "Supervisors" to "Team Leaders". The second change was most important. The word "supervisor" intimates that the people need to be watched over because we don't trust them, whereas "Team Leader" is someone who is a leader of a team of people. A subtle but important difference.

We also asked the previously named "supervisors" if they wanted to attend leadership training night classes, to which everyone signed up.

All important changes to make to the organisation to facilitate the start of changing culture.

As we draw this chapter to a close, I would advise you to think of Candour like a muscle – in the sense that you need to train it!

Trust me, learning to build this muscle will be one of the best things you've ever done and as you make that clear to the entire organisation, things will only get better.

Stop being comfortable with dysfunction; start to develop a "stop" culture. When you see a struggle or things not going the way you would like, stop and reflect on what needs to change, always starting with yourself and taking action to fix it.

Even the most natural of lean leaders need to practise this, as when things are not going the way you'd like, our natural tendency is to ask, "Why are they not doing X, Y, or Z?" Remember that the first response from a lean leader when a situation like this arises is, "Am I doing it?" or building on that further: "Have I created the conditions for X, Y, or Z to happen?" "Have I created clarity around that expectation?" "Have I just 'told them', or have I provided a clear documented process?" Rarely is the answer to all these questions truthfully "yes".

You can't sell what you haven't really bought into yourself.

That includes how you are doing with building your lean culture. It's never about "them"; it's always about you.

Improvement starts with I and Candour starts with I. Don't forget it!

Here's where Candour starts

- Candour has four stages: STOP, SPEAK UP, LISTEN, ACT. Creating a safe space for your organisation to act this way is a big part of lean.
- Examine yourself and your team and commit that you will do whatever it takes to "change the people or change the people".
- Look at your KPIs and incentive methods. Do any actively work against lean?

CHAPTER 2

The Second "C" – COMMITMENT

"The quality of a person's life is in direct proportion to their commitment to excellence, regardless of their chosen field of endeavour."
— Vince Lombardi

Nothing worthwhile in life can be bought or delegated. Not your physical health, not a skill or an aptitude, not a beautiful relationship, nor an outstanding company culture. An analogy I used with a recent client who makes high-end gym equipment (that you will become more familiar with later), after they had visited Seating Matters and wanted the same culture, was that this is like going to the gym and seeing some guy with a 12 pack of abs, a world-class physique. You decide you want the same, so you get a world-class coach to train you. That's great: the coach can advise you of the right steps to take to reach your goal, the exercise regime, the diet, and can even shout at you when you need motivation. Super! The unfortunate truth is, though, that only you can lift the weights. Only you can decide to eat clean and not eat the cheeseburger. Only you can make and keep the Commitment to change. Only you can build your culture. Commitment starts with "I".

That guy with the world-class physique, with the 12 pack of abdominals, didn't get it by just popping into the gym for a few half hours of half-assed workouts a week or by wolfing down a pizza after a dozen beers every other night, did he? No. You only get to be world-class at ANYTHING if that is your number 1 priority. If it's something you approach among your many "priorities", it's highly unlikely that you will get outstanding results.

Interestingly, the word "priority" was only used in the singular until the middle of the 20th century. Before that, the very essence of the word meant that there could only be one. We've been fooled into thinking that the word "priorities" is plural, which leads to a proliferation of multitasking and a lot of bland performance.

When I look at someone like Paul Akers or Ryan Tierney or, frankly, anyone with one of those truly, top-of-the-league lean organisations, I reckon that if you cut the leaders in half, it stays lean. They live and breathe lean all the time. Total Commitment. They are all extremely candid people consumed with improvement and, as I said earlier, start first by improving what stares back in the mirror: themselves. Without a doubt, lean is their top priority, yet they are not "one-trick ponies". Paul is a brilliant leader, a great business strategist, amazing sales guy, great public speaker, and voracious reader. He not only has an amazing company, but he has also done IronMan numerous times, travelled to over 100 countries, is a pilot, and has climbed to Everest Base Camp and Kilimanjaro, and on and on and on...

How do you do all that?

When you decide to make a Commitment to growing a world-class lean culture, the thing to realise is that you

are NOT saying no to lots of other things; you are just saying a whole-hearted YES to first taking your personal development seriously and devoting time to that so that you can be a world-class leader within your organisation, so, in turn, it can become a world-class company with world-class people, processes, and products.

For most of you reading this book, If you don't say "yes" to building a lean culture, you are saying YES to continuing dysfunction and mediocrity with an organisational environment that shouts average at everything it encounters. For 98% of people, that is their business life. It might be a "nice environment" with "good results", but is it outstanding? Is it something truly spectacular? Would people want to travel from all over the world to learn how you do things at your place? The answer is likely to be a resounding NO if you don't make a significant change to how you manage yourself and those around you. I'm going to quote Einstein again, and his applicable quote here is: "The definition of insanity is doing the same thing over and over again whilst expecting different results".

A good question to ask about why you would want to commit to Lean is, **"Why do you actually want a lean organisation at all?"**

There are **good reasons and not so good reasons** that, again, will help you understand if this is for you. Many answers are on the "right" side of the spectrum to this question, just a few of which we can start to look at here.

I want a world-class company. I want that positive energy that world-class lean organisations have.

I want to eliminate the stress and struggle that comes with having a disorganised mess, with all the firefighting that goes with it, never being able to take a break, the poor quality of home life that goes with that, and so on.

Ultimately, **some unmet psychological need is driving you to want change**. The bigger the need, the more motivation you are fuelled with to change.

I "got" 2 Second Lean immediately because, in my first company, the ownership team were pressuring me to "implement lean", and it was **the only way** I could see to accomplish the transformation.

For Ryan Tierney of Seating Matters, he was so stressed out trying to run the factory that he Googled "how do I run a factory?" and came across Paul Akers' videos on YouTube. He was hooked immediately. He saw 2 Second Lean as **the only way** to solve his problems, and he didn't have many options available at that time!

For Paul Vallely of Kukoon Rugs (another amazing 2 Second Lean company from Northern Ireland), it was greeting people who worked for him and receiving no response or a grunt. He did not want to spend his life working in that kind of dull, impersonal, lifeless environment where there were no connections and warmth within his organisation. He sees 2 Second Lean as **the best wa**y to solve his problem.

The specific reason might be different for many other lean leaders I know, but the outcome was the same: they saw 2 Second Lean as **THE vehicle to transport them from a situation of discomfort to one of a better place.** When they started to apply 2 Second Lean principles, they gave it their full and singular focus.

Frankly speaking, the bigger the pain, the greater the burning desire you have for your goal, the better. If you don't have a genuine burning desire at the heart of your motivation to build a lean culture, then you will likely give up when the going gets tough, as it most definitely will at some point. A "burning boat" certainly helps leaders make and keep to their Commitment.

When I analyse those business leaders that don't bother with lean, those people that visit lean organisations, get blown away at what those companies achieve, but then go on to do nothing substantive themselves, I see three main reasons that lie behind their behaviour.

The first is that they don't understand what they are seeing.

They see the physical improvements, witness the efficient working environment, communication boards, and slick processes, and think that is what they have to do. They try to copy the outcome, not what made it happen, which is focusing on growing people and building a culture that delivers those improvements. Just trying to copy the results will fall flat on its face 99.9 times out of 100.

The second reason is that they don't have enough discomfort in their current situation.

Life could be good – maybe not brilliant or world-class, but there is not a big enough fire in the belly to find out more and move into action. Either that, or it's the excuse mindset mentioned earlier in the Candour chapter. In any case, the result is zero Commitment to change.

Good is the enemy of excellent. Comfort does not stimulate transformative change; pain does. So, without perceiving a substantive reason to make that change, most leaders will choose the current status quo or make small, safe changes that don't go beyond the superficial in terms of culture change.

In other words, they see options. Often lots of them! All of them easier than doing this "lean thing" that they don't really understand.

That is the third reason: they don't know what to do next.

Well, that is why this book was written! To give people a bridge to build from curiosity into action.

Back to *motivations* of those you who are considering moving forward with lean – on the "not so good" side of answers to the motivation question are those that sound like this:

"I want to make more money" or, alternatively, "I want to get more out of my people", or "I want more for less". The financial motivation is okay if it is at the lower end of your list of unmet needs, but if it is at the top of your list, forget it.

Your people are not stupid. If you are using lean as just another way to manipulate and exploit them more, they will sniff that out in short shrift, and the whole thing will monumentally fail. That is one of the reasons why lean often fails to get real, authentic buy-in within large corporations. **Leaders are doing it not because they want to but because they've been told to do it.** It's about delivering the KPIs and the weekly, monthly, and quarterly results. It's all about results and improvements without understanding that the engagement drives those other things, those end results. There is no heart behind doing it; it's just another corporate tool and, in the worst examples, just "another thing" that corporate are piling on to an already stressed-out organisation.

The thing is, every single REAL lean organisation that I know makes money for fun – like serious, serious coin compared to their competitors – and there's a very simple reason for that. It's because truly lean companies are very rare, and it's highly unlikely they have a competitor in their segment anywhere near as good as them. The excellent lean organisations have a fully **engaged** group of people highly **motivated to remove waste from everything they do**, every day, with a **servant attitude** to their customers, totally focussed on delivering **excellent value and service to their customers every single day.**

Does your business do that? At that kind of level of intensity?

What do you think would happen to your results if it did?

Think about that and consider what attitudes you might have to work on changing.

The thing is, for lean to work, it needs to come from the heart and speak to people's souls, not their wallets.

It's sad but obvious: everyone wants better, but very few are willing to change themselves first and then sustain that change long enough for the results to come.

That is the second Commitment you are making here: that whatever it takes, you are going to do it, and you are not going to give up. I can tell you right now that you ARE going to hit a few speed bumps along the way because you are on a new road of discovery. True lean leaders hold onto their vision and keep going regardless, making adjustments but always with forward momentum. The best leaders enjoy the journey and understand that the undoubted challenges are an essential part of it. **The growth is actually hidden in those challenges**

because, by overcoming them, you and the organisation grow.

To illustrate this spirit, let me give you an example of my very first day of "proper" 2 Second Lean. After several months of working hard to convince the company's ownership team to "just do it", I was mid-way through my very first Morning Meeting, full of enthusiasm for this amazing change, when it dawned on me that a good half of the 50 people in the audience had no clue at all what I was saying.

Blank faces stared back at me.

A good half of those people didn't understand English, as they were foreign nationals with barely a rudimentary grasp of the language.

I hid my shock well and kept going, maintaining a good front for the rest of the day, but driving back home that evening in the car, I was really worried.

What do I do with this? Will we be able to do this 2 Second Lean thing at all? I felt like a total fool. After all this arm-wrestling and convincing with the senior team, changing the payment structure and selling to every single individual how great lean was going to be, was this project going to die before we even got started? I had put my reputation totally on the line here. The truth was that I'd already gone too far. The Commitment was already too great for me to go back. My "reputation boat" had been well and truly burned!

In hindsight, that was a really good thing.

I actually prayed.

Then it hit me:

USE THE PROBLEM AS AN OPPORTUNITY.

I got it straight away.

I'd simplify all the communication, no more than a dozen words on any single presentation slide, and I used Google Translate to convert the text into SIX different languages: English, Polish, Lithuanian, Bulgarian, Latvian, and Hungarian, and I kept the education part as visual as possible. I also slowed down the education part of the Morning Meeting dramatically. I went much slower than I normally did, but it gave more time for the learning to sink in.

EXPRESSING GRATITUDE

Išreikškite dėkingumą

HATÁSAI / Wdzięczny / KĻŪT PAR GALĪGU / БЪДЕТE ВЕЛИКИ

Eng / Lith / Hun / Pol / Lat / Bul

An example of one of my Morning Meeting slides

I began with this approach the very next day, and right away, it started to work like a treat. I asked Ramunas or one of the other good English speakers to translate other parts of what we were talking about into Russian or Lithuanian, and every meeting from then on, I made a real point of doing this. I would actually use it as a crutch if the meeting was falling a bit flat or getting a bit boring to stimulate some interaction and levity.

I was very deliberate about including even the shy and retiring people, who were nervous about speaking (imagine the fear that many have about public speaking but now multiply that because it's not your mother tongue!), to make contributions.

For our Book Club, every day, I posted translations from Google Translate and copied and pasted from the PDF foreign language versions of *2 Second Lean* into our company WhatsApp group so that everyone had an opportunity to learn. Of course, the translations weren't perfect, but that was half of the fun. Every individual had to do a Book Club slot in the Morning Meeting. If their language was not up to it, one of their friends could translate it into English for them for the group. It stretched everyone but brought them out of their comfort zone and into the group dynamic.

Later, I asked for a translator volunteer called Normunds, who would translate and explain key messages into Russian, which was the language most of the foreign guys could understand.

It all really worked.

I reckon the reason is that I showed that I truly cared about every single person in the organisation and that no one who wanted to come with us on this journey would be left behind. Before this, for many of the foreign nationals, management didn't actually know their real name, so it was a night and day difference.

Getting ready for a Morning Meeting at
my first 2 Second Lean company

It was a heck of a lot of hard work for me personally, but it was certainly worth it. **If I had not given it 100% Commitment, I would have failed.** Honestly, I think 9 out of 10 people would have given up at this first hurdle, but I just would not. I refused.

You can see some videos of what we achieved below.

GT Investni Operational Excellence
https://youtu.be/1ic_Kcu-fTY

GT INVESTNI OPERATIONAL EXCELLENCE

Tom Hughes Lumen GembaDocs Lean

GT Best Day of improvements ever!
https://youtu.be/99b-opXwXRQ

GT BEST DAY OF IMPROVEMENTS!

Tom Hughes Lumen GembaDocs Lean

GT Happy New Year Transformation
https://youtu.be/SQ2TUWby6Fs

GT Happy New Year Transformation

Tom Hughes Lumen GembaDocs Lean

I can sincerely tell you that I personally got huge growth out of the whole experience and also that those Morning Meetings and Improvement Times were some of the happiest times in my career, just watching people blossom. The organisation also exponentially grew as a team. It was fantastic.

But it all grew out of what, for many, would have been a seemingly insurmountable obstacle, and that's why it takes some serious Commitment for everyone to be truly great at lean. "Can't" can be translated as "won't" in many situations.

The rest of what I talk about in this chapter is just helping you overcome some of the rational barriers you might have built up to saying "Yes" to that Commitment.

Committing to lean does not mean that your business can't grow sales at an extraordinary pace, that you can't have a cash focus, or product development can't be a key differentiator for your business if any of those things are strategically important to you. If you are an entrepreneur and you truly love lean, it will take away all the operational firefighting rubbish that means you can be stuck well and truly "in the business". Instead, you can work "on the business", and you get to go kitesurfing for a couple of months in South America while your well-oiled machine just gets on with what it does with a light touch from you. (Paul Akers can do stuff like this!). I've often said to people that if your business doesn't function without you standing in it every day, you aren't a true business owner – you have a job in a business that you happen to own. I recently came across a quotation that stated something very similar but added, "And your boss is a psychopath..."

What's important to understand is that, no matter the primary outcome you are after for your business, lean can be the vehicle that gets you there. To repeat what we said earlier, "Everything in life is a process or the outcome of a process", so **lean in itself**

is not the end, but it's a fantastic means to get to whatever end you seek. The focus is always continuous improvement, and that will improve all your people and processes constantly. If your competition is not doing the same, you can only develop a competitive advantage, with better people, processes, products, or services.

When you make a Commitment to lean, you need to understand that the process of creating a lean culture is all about pull, with only a little bit of push.

The pull starts with YOU becoming the lean practitioner, the "triple X leader", who is the exceptional, extraordinary example every day. That means you are actively making improvements every single day within your own span of control. This means raising your own standards and addressing the problems you face every day, big and small. It means developing your own "stop culture" and living and breathing it at a high level all the time.

This is your #1 Commitment, and it starts with I, not with pointing the finger at other people. If you truly embrace this, you cannot fail.

I first encountered this kind of leader when I was in Japan with Mr Akers.

In spite of all the early exposure to Japanese companies that I had the good fortune to have in the early part of my career, plus the fact that I've travelled all over the world, visiting over 50 countries, I'd never been to Japan. It was completely amazing to be exposed to that beautiful culture and environment for the first time. Everything was just better than home! You can see some of the videos I made during the trip in this chapter. Let's just say that the people just blew me away with their mutual respect for each other, and the attitude to detail and quality everywhere in the country left a lasting impression on me. It won't be the last time I go there.

Anyhow, what impressed me even more was being around Paul himself. He is a force of nature. He genuinely loves imparting his wisdom to others; it certainly is not about just making money for him. His Candour is totally off the chart. If something isn't working, he has a very sensitive trigger to sense it and take action. He constantly improved everything around him, all the time. He never stopped. It wasn't a study mission about lean; it was a lean study mission! He wasn't just preaching lean, he was doing it, and he clearly loved sharing that knowledge with others so that they could make their lives better. I made a short video on the "difference between Paul Akers and normal people" that summarises these differences when I was at the airport home from Japan.

The difference between Paul Akers and a normal person https://youtu.be/Lhx1BKowh-Y

Fukuoka Airport...

The difference between Paul Akers and a normal person

Tom Hughes Lumen GembaDocs Lean

Anyhow, back to the Japan lean study mission.

One of the best improvements was around how we managed the personal headset intercoms we all wore as we went around factories on tour so that we could hear each other. Most people would just have put them into a box when we were done, with that just becoming a tangled mess of wires. Instead of having everyone randomly return them back with wires hanging everywhere, Paul created a quality standard of how the wire would be wrapped around each one to reduce all the excess motion around all the wires becoming tangled. He then presented the new standard to us on PowerPoint on the bus to communicate so that we all knew about the standard, helping us understand that EVERYTHING IS A PROCESS!

Paul on the bus – EVERYTHING IS A PROCESS
https://youtu.be/X5xhJ-wQMu4

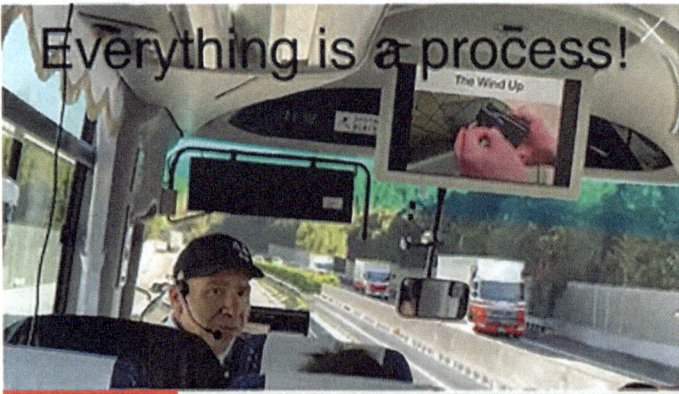

Paul on the bus - EVERYTHING IS A PROCESS!

Tom Hughes Lumen GembaDocs Lean

Then his assistant Mami-San came up with the idea of putting a number on each one to further reduce the struggle. It was amazing.

The Lean Bus 071119
https://youtu.be/7TdnIpHJqJc

The LEAN Bus! 071119

Tom Hughes Lumen GembaDocs Lean

I asked Paul, "How many improvements do you make a day?" His answer was, "Around 30 or 40", and having seen him in action, I believed him.

I wanted some of that juice, that Kool-Aid that Paul was very evidently drinking. I resolved to myself: I made a Commitment that I'm going to make at least five improvements a day from now on.

About three days later, on the last day of the tour, I had failed abysmally. Literally not one improvement made! We were having lunch before the last afternoon of the trip – a visit to the Holy Grail of the Lexus plant. I told Paul about my failure. Well, at least I was Candid!

I asked him, "How do you do it? How do you see all those improvements?" Again, I was fortunate enough to capture his response on video, which is linked below. However, to summarise, he said that ANY time he experiences struggle or sees things bunching up in a bottleneck, there it is. That is an opportunity for improvement.

How Paul Akers sees opportunities to improve
https://youtu.be/kB_qbOTgWvY

How Paul Akers sees opportunities to improve

Tom Hughes Lumen GembaDocs Lean

To be honest, I'd heard similar things from different people and other sources in the past, but this time, something was different; a switch tripped of understanding that has stayed and been refined until this day.

Every time we see a struggle or things not flowing, there is an opportunity for improvement.

It has been 118 weeks since that day, and I've made at least 25 improvements per week since then. I track and record them all in a fantastic habit-building app called "Done". It's the most important app tool in my life. I use it to build and sustain habits by holding myself accountable, to hold myself to that Commitment. There's a video on how I use the app below.

How I use the Done app
https://youtu.be/Z7nDFGMFHK8

The Done App - creating and sustaining habits and impro...

Tom Hughes Lumen GembaDocs Lean

When you do that, when you are a triple X leader consistently, you will become a magnet, pulling your team with you. Eventually, all those who get it will be drawn to follow, and those who don't will fall away. Any who actively resist is where the little bit of push might come in. My friend Ryan Tierney at Seating Matters put it best when he said that lean leaders need to be sheepdogs, not bulldogs. The lean leader is not the bulldog rushing into the middle of the flock barking, shouting, and biting, being loud and egotistical, scattering the flock everywhere. The lean leader does not try to push anyone into doing lean; they are an altogether smarter beast than that!

The sheepdog gently guides the flock (their people!) for the vast majority of the time. The flock hardly knows that they are there, but they go along with the flow of the others. The sheepdog is constantly vigilant, making sure everyone is going in the right direction. If one or two go the wrong way, he makes his presence felt with a look, a bark, or even a nipped bite so they can correct their course. The flock can go long distances under the guidance of a good sheepdog, but before they even know it, they are in the pen, and it's all over!

That is the Commitment you need to make a decision on. That is what you need to be asking yourself. Am I prepared to be the sheepdog? Am I the one who does that?

Andries Overweg, a Lean Maniac from the Netherlands who was one of the people who helped me edit this book, has made an excellent video illustrating the "sheepdog principle":

Lead like a sheepdog
https://youtu.be/XW8rOeKVNwU

Lead like a sheepdog

Andries Overweg

Every single exceptional lean culture company needs at least one lean leader – or, put alternatively, a lean zealot – that person who gets excited about the smallest improvement and enjoys celebrating that, yet is always positively dissatisfied, looking for improvement opportunities. The lean zealot will be the one who loses sleep if lean isn't going well, and he will never, ever give up. They have made that 100% personal Commitment. Paul Akers calls these people the 2% – those who truly "get" lean.

This person is the one who says, "Great, now what?", challenging the organisation to ever greater heights. That person doesn't HAVE to be the owner or the CEO, but it definitely helps. If they aren't occupying that role, they certainly need to have a number 2 or 3 position and for it to be clear to all that the lean culture is the priority and that they have serious authority to make decisions around resources and hiring and firing as a minimum. If that individual has to go running to someone else to approve buying a box of paperclips, it is not a good look. They need organisational credibility. Otherwise, it's another serious iceberg that could put a serious hole in the hull of your lean ship on its journey.

When you decide to make a Commitment to lean, you are deciding that your company will be doing Morning Meetings and 3s (Sweep, Sort, Standardise) activities every day forever, or at least for the foreseeable future. This is not what I call "traditional lean" with "events/kaizen events" happening sporadically and then everyone gets back to work. I've never seen that breed a truly amazing culture personally. If lean is not an everyday activity, with quality time given to making it a focus, the continuous improvement culture never takes hold and, like Paul Akers says in his book, makes you feel like you are constantly "pushing a train". It's a struggle to even maintain standards, never mind constantly improving them. Still, for many people, this idea of having the guts of an hour a day not focused on making stuff or delivering your service is completely alien. How does that pay for itself?

When I did my first lean transformation, it was a serious problem for me as a lean leader to convince the other senior people, who were actually the owners of the company, that it was a good idea to have their 50 staff stand around for half an hour in this meeting and then another half an hour 3s'ing and making improvements. For them, that was easily $700 a day, without a widget being hit. These were hard-nosed people. What's in it for them? Plus they're busy, with overtime already to meet customer demand, and we want them to stop making stuff for an hour a day?

I can tell you that this was not an easy obstacle initially for me. I was lucky (as I often am!) when discussing the matter with one of my best friends, Nic Jameron, whom I originally met when he was recruited as the production manager when I was running a factory in France. He is a brilliant leader, production manager and supply chain guy.

Nic Jameron & I during our Olaer days

When I was discussing 2SL with him and telling him about my "convincing the team" challenge, he said it was easy to understand. "What?" I said. He explained it in his very French way: that it was simple. "All you need to do in an eight-hour shift is to get 15% better, and that hour is free forever". I'd never thought about it that way, but it's true. At that organisation, we got a 24% productivity improvement within five months, and that was including the "lost hour". That was just the start.

So, making this Commitment has logic: **it might take a month or two, but it won't be long before that investment has been permanently paid back.**

You also don't have to do a full hour. Depending on the context, I recommend to my coaching clients currently that they start with 10 or 15 minutes and just see where it goes in terms of adding value for them. Half an hour is required, however, for 3s'ing and making those improvements.

In most organisations with a physical dimension to their process, it is very rare that we even have to find the whole 45 minutes. Unless there is a constraint such as health and safety, just eliminate end of shift cleaning, which I've seen can be 45 minutes of relaxing time in many companies, where a broom is casually pushed around and there is a proliferation of people running off for smoke breaks. Rarely is there any real management oversight at these times, so stop that completely, run the machines until the last minute, and then clock off.

First thing then is the Morning Meeting for the entire company and 3S improvement time, which includes the cleaning, but this half-hour has a whole level of management or team leaders present on the Gemba coaching, helping, and supporting their people in their cleaning and improvement activities. So, even this time Commitment is rarely "*le mer a boire*", as my French buddy would say. This means it's "not the sea to drink!"

So far, we have focused on the "why" of Commitment for decision-makers, the people at the higher end of an organisation chart. However, for lean to work, everyone in the organisation needs to have a genuine personal reason to engage with it, an actual benefit that will accrue to them personally, the WIIFM (the "What's In It For Me?").

This came up quite by accident when I was invited to my first consultant-client company meeting. The Managing Director was giving a state of the nation address, supported by other members of the leadership team. I wasn't expecting to be introduced or asked to speak, but it happened: I was put on the spot and pulled right out of my comfort zone!

After a short introduction, I launched into a series of questions to the audience and asked them to raise their hands and keep them raised if the answer was "yes".

I asked these questions:

Who would like less stress in their day-to-day work lives?

Who would like less friction between departments?

Who would like happier customers?

Who would like to struggle less every day?

As this went on, more and more hands went up and stayed up. My objective was to get the entire room with raised hands.

Who would like to make more money?

Who would like to be tapping their steering wheel driving here because it's just such a great place to work?

There was a great atmosphere in the room, and when all hands were raised, I said, "Brilliant. Thanks everyone! Every single one of us now has a reason to want to do lean". All very "I'm Spartacus!" (you'll know what I mean if you've seen the classic Kirk Douglas):

"I'm Spartacus" scene from the classic 1960s Hollywood movie *Spartacus*
https://youtu.be/FKCmyiljKo0

I'm Spartacus - Spartacus (8/10) Movie CLIP (1960) HD

Movieclips

But especially in these early days, we need signals to the organisation that things are changing and that this serious.

Just as a fun note, if I'd kept asking questions and was still getting one or two hands staying down, my last question was going to be: "Do you want to work here?", and if they'd still kept their hands down, I'd have asked them to leave, perhaps not very ceremoniously. That would take us back to Candour…

As we draw to a close on the Commitment chapter, I'd like to point out that for many, verbal and mental commitments are very easy to make. Like at New Year, when we say we're going to give up this or take up that new habit or make that change, how many of us actually make it into concrete, real actions that last?

Let's just say, not many.

We have a few sayings in lean that apply here.

The first comes from Taiichi Ohno, who was instrumental in creating the Toyota Production System. Some would say he was "the Father of Lean": "The best improvement is the one that you can do right now". Another that helps us along to the same understanding is one I first heard from Paul Akers' company, FastCap's lean principles, but apparently originally came from Winston Churchill: "Action. This day".

So, from what we have examined so far in the Candour and Commitment chapters, what action(s) are you taking today?

- REAL lean culture starts with "I". To be successful, leaders have to be "sheepdogs" and lead by setting a very high standard of actually practising lean for it to work.

- Every single person in the organisation needs to understand that lean is not about waiting for everyone else to change; it is about all of us, as individuals being high-level examples.

- Lean is not a "means to an end" but a vehicle you can use to take your organisation wherever you want it to go.

CHAPTER 3

The Third "C" – COACHING

> **"A great coach tells you what you need to hear, not what you want to hear."**
> — **Sagi Kalev**

Every organisation that successfully implements 2 Second Lean has at least one world-class coach within their core team, often the leader of the company but not necessarily so. Whether those individuals started their lean journeys as world-class coaches is highly unlikely. Therefore, to grow their respective organisations, they had to learn to become great coaches along the way.

Without a doubt, the best way to develop your coaching skills is by starting to coach yourself. Coaching starts with I.

The only problem with that approach is that if you are not naturally gifted and just go at it like a bull in a china shop, you might have a company full of half-broken people within a very short space of time. The biggest pitfall is if you don't fully understand pull vs push and therefore try to manipulate or coerce your people into "doing lean", which can irreparably damage the whole lean transformation before it has even started.

I had my own set of trials and errors in helping others come on board with lean within my companies where I was a senior leader, but it was only when I started coaching other companies on lean that I was able to develop a very clear and deliberate framework to establish an actual process to get full-on engagement to the lean process.

That process has now been tested and will act as a set of stabilisers to help you go about getting your lean implementation off to a good start or provide a basis for you to renew your current efforts if your company has been doing lean for a long time. After all, everything is a process or the outcome of a process, including how you "do lean".

The whole idea of me coaching lean with other companies happened completely by accident.

It happened because my first 2 Second Lean company transformation was an exceptional example, and it received some good publicity in a relatively short time. As a result, I was asked to present on the "how did we do it?" at a conference for an important organisation, Manufacturing NI. I had a real ball doing that. I have enjoyed performing in front of crowds since I was a boy performing music and playing in bands. In addition, on this occasion, my genuine passion for the subject shone through.

I began to garner a good reputation locally in Ireland for seeming to know what I was doing in the space. However, "musical differences" meant that I parted company with that original organisation, although thankfully on good terms with the ownership team.

Around this time, the coronavirus was just starting to make an impact, and the whole world seemed to be on lockdown. These were strange times. In a typical lean guy fashion, though, I was still seeing struggle everywhere, and a notable one at the time was how local supermarkets were really struggling to make the whole hand sanitiser thing work. It was actually hard to get hold of the stuff at the beginning, and on one visit to my local store, I watched two staff members struggling to decant fluid from one plastic bottle to another with the liquid going all over the place. Within struggle lies opportunity, so after a short space of time, I found myself working with fellow Lean Maniac Patrick Magee of Lumen Electronics – another company practising 2 Second Lean – whom I had visited earlier that year. Patrick and I had hit it off and became buddies. We had chatted about "if the opportunity ever came up to work on a product together", and here it was. We were developing a sanitiser dispenser.

With the help of our other partner, James McGilloway on mechanical design, we launched the first version in record time, from idea to product in about six weeks (seriously!). I had already found a great route to market, and we quickly sold over one thousand of the things to retailers all over the UK and Ireland. Things looked good!

Then they started to come back. There were some serious problems with how robust the design was versus the rigours of the application. It wasn't much fun for the next few months with constant field issues, refurbishments, and replacements.

Still, through the adversity, Patrick and I came to respect each other more and became fast friends. Many would have tried to cut and run or get off the hook because it was truly painful. Not us. Together with James, we developed a "GEN2" version of the product, which is truly world-class being sold all over the world, restoring our reputations and making those original customers happy with their purchases. It was something I took very much to heart as I'd never been involved with something that had gone so wrong before. GEN2 was much more about repaying our customers' faith in us than it was ever about making money.

Towards the end of 2020, I told Patrick that I intended to go into business coaching as it was something I just loved doing, when Patrick responded, "Why don't you do that for us?" That initiative turned into Patrick and I deciding to go into partnership in Lumen Electronics together, as our skill sets really complemented each other well. Me for the strategy, commercial, management, and mechanical stuff, and Patrick being the electronic guru. Both of us are crazy about lean.

So, we started lifting Lumen to new heights on everything we did. We developed a new strategy of "Total Product Management", where we handled cradle to grave product development, from proof of concept through to mass production, from electronics, mechanical, and even software development. It's unique for anyone – in Ireland, at least – and so far, it's working great.

The Lumen Electronics Website
https://www.lumen-electronics.com/

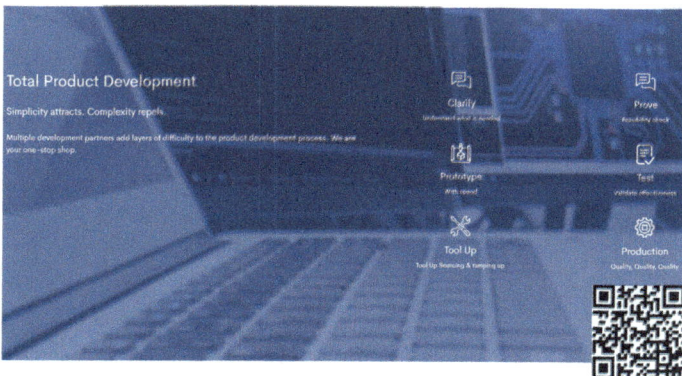

Me at Lumen with Patrick (right) and John McKenna (left)

While we are forever positively dissatisfied with what is happening at Lumen, it is turning into a shining example of what lean can do within a small company environment. We even recently hosted the world-renowned AME 2 Second Lean Tour with Paul Akers and Richard Evans:

Lumen AME Lean Tour
https://youtu.be/x9VHPyyJGsE

Lumen Electronics AME #8 Tour

FastCap

It was a resounding success. We now get customers asking us how they can replicate what they see at our place, which is turning into a source of coaching clients for yours truly, and while Lumen is still small, I have time to give other companies, which is a happy situation.

During this time, I also became good buddies with other people in the lean space, like Ryan Tierney. They have companies visiting them for lean tours all the time, and I've been turning into the "go-to person" for people looking for help.

My first "proper" coaching client was a company called BLK BOX from Belfast, who make and sell high-end fitness gear. These are the guys I mentioned in the previous chapter. Their managing director, Greg Bradley, is a visionary in the fitness industry who started the company from nothing. They had visited Seating Matters prior to COVID kicking off and got excited about lean, but their lean ambitions were side-lined by the minor distraction of a global pandemic...

Now things were calming down on that front, and in the meantime, they had doubled in size and taken a bunch of manufacturing processes in-house that had previously been outsourced. They were looking for some help as things had become somewhat chaotic.

Initially, when Greg approached me, he asked for someone to support getting his manufacturing into a better state. I explained there were probably a dozen people better in Northern Ireland to talk to about that, but if he wanted someone to coach him to help build a lean culture, then I would be really excited about doing that.

I had previously been approached by a large local concrete company with more than 1000 employees to help them build a lean culture. I had put in a lot of work to develop a methodology for them to use, but in the end, I was disappointed when they didn't go for it. Their mountains of waste are highly likely to still be there to this day.

I discussed that opportunity with Paul Akers, who in that time, had also turned into a friend, mentor, and surrogate father figure to me – as he would remind me, a very young father!

He helped me put that initial framework together, so I was dying to try it out. I was delighted that Greg agreed for me to come and help BLK BOX become a world-class lean company. The guys were paying me to do this coaching job, but for me, it was never about the money; it was always about helping them grow into a world-class organisation. My goal was quite contrary to a traditional consultant who wants to get lots of paid days at the company. I wanted to help them get momentum, for their lean process to become self-sustaining, and to get out as soon as possible.

I am happy to report that this is exactly what happened. The time with BLK BOX helped me prove this framework and improve it. To my mind, this framework could work for almost all organisations with or without an external coach like me who has done it before.

Personally, though, I recommend going the external coach route. Someone like myself who has "done it" multiple times certainly does help avoid some of the hard pitfalls that are created by "soft issues" (boy, do I hate that term!). Soft issues are (not "can be") the difference between bad and outstanding. The soft issues are about leadership, skilful management, and culture building. They are the foundation and cause for the "hard numbers" – whether those numbers are bad or exceptionally good!

My initial discussions with Greg had a lot to do with the Candour and Commitment chapters we have already covered. As an external coach, it was critical to me that my role was well defined. I was here to advise, cajole, and support but not to lift the weights. Only the leadership team could do that.

There are several critical advantages that an external coach has over just using an internal resource.

The first is that the external coach provides a new set of eyes, a fresh perspective to the organisation. Some of those less-than-smart practises – like the non-productive meetings that everyone has got used to but no one speaks up about or the management team member with the bad attitude that everyone else has learnt to just put up with – the external coach can spot the obvious and surface those issues to leadership. It often provokes them into action, where even they had become comfortable with the dysfunction before.

It's even better when the external coach has broad and deep experience to provide a good mirror, especially when the leaders have spent a long time immersed in a single organisation. This is especially true in an owner-grown company, where the leader has not been heavily exposed to best practises from other organisations/sectors. The external coach can provide a great stimulus to look at things in a different way.

The external coach gets to call things as they see them without being perceived as being partisan in any way. It's harder for an internal person to do that without being seen as having personal baggage or them being fearful about upsetting people too much when difficult things need to be said, especially when that communication is to the top management.

A great external coach can be a Consilieri; the last thing you want is a consultant...

With Greg, I put together a roadmap on how I would support the team to get up and running. It was going to take four to six weeks before we would start the Morning Meetings, and these were the key steps in the run up to that.

Step 1: Who will be the "Ryan?"

You might ask, what does that mean?

The answer is simple: from observing companies from all over the world, and especially the ones that have lean done right, it's evident that at every company, there is a **clear leader for lean**, whether that be Ryan Tierney at Seating Matters (that's why I use the term "Ryan" here), Paul Akers at Fastcap, or my friend Brannon Burton at Sunroc Corporation, there is always a clear and visible lean leader.

Now, they are always supported by some other exceptional lean leaders who have developed alongside those guys, but there is always someone clear at the top who is clearly accountable for the whole culture and its effectiveness.

Very few things are done well by the committee, so saying, **"We are all accountable" simply doesn't work**. No one person is lying awake at night wondering what to do when lean hits a rocky patch, OR is lying awake, excited with a new idea to try out to make things even better. There simply has to be a single individual, a lynchpin holding the whole thing together.

At BLK BOX, the "Ryan" was agreed to be a chap called Peter McCauley, who was head of manufacturing. Peter was a senior member of the leadership team and had a passion for lean and developing people. He was an ideal choice. He had the clear and visible support of Greg and the other senior leaders within that team.

Step 2: Establish a "Learning Club"

The objective of the Learning Club is to get the senior team practising lean on a daily basis THEMSELVES within their sphere of influence and starting to "pull not push" their teams on board. We want to turn this group into a team of internal coaches. The idea is to create a magnet of excitement/excellence that gets other people curious about what is happening.

Curiosity was something I was learning about at the time through someone I knew who had a child with autism, specifically a condition called PDA (Pathological Demand Avoidance). Children with this condition cannot deal with the traditional school system, reacting badly to any kind of order, demand, or even a request. It pushes them into anxiety, and they can react in all kinds of ways, few of them particularly positive. No kind of traditional carrot and stick type of parenting works. I listened to an expert talk on the subject, and he said the key to learning for PDA people was curiosity. **If curiosity can be created, a space is made for learning to happen.** It occurred to me that this was not just for people with PDA; it's true for all of us. Many of us have crammed for an academic examination that we just needed to pass with rote learning only to forget it all after a few days. However, if the topic of learning is something we are genuinely curious about, it becomes an automatic, self-motivated process. This is key and one of the important factors in creating pull.

The Learning Club helps set new expectations at an early stage. Everyone has to make improvements and get on board as we set the tone with the leadership team for how lean is done. This is not just the traditional "top-down management commitment" that translates in most organisations to the senior management just "supporting" the rest of the company to do it but actually not doing it themselves. This is how most organisations change initiatives are "pushed" into a company and has been the normal *modus operandus* for decades. **It's also why the vast majority of organisational change initiatives fail to get traction or sustain. When you step back and look at this normal way of doing things, it fails because it's hypocritical. "Do as I say, not as I do".**

This point cannot be emphasised enough. Everyone, especially senior leaders, needs to stop being "carpet walkers". In a manufacturing environment, that means getting your hands dirty by getting out onto the shopfloor where the work is done. Regularly, every single day.

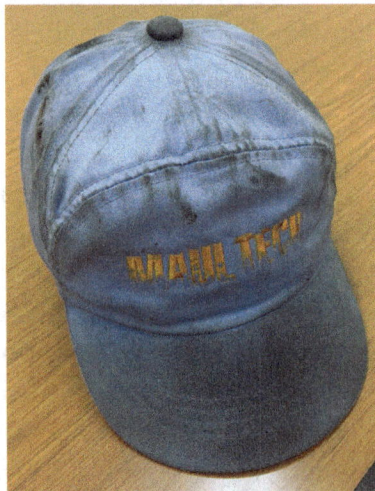

A leader's hat – I took this photo during the Japan study mission. It belonged to the owner of a $30m company, Maul Tech. He was certainly not afraid of getting his hands dirty

Paul Akers recently responded to a bunch of senior executives from a multi-billion-dollar company who asked him what the most important thing they could do to "implement lean" was by telling them to **"get their heads out of their asses and get on to the shopfloor and work side by side with their people".** Not what those guys are used to hearing!

For those not in manufacturing departments or whose business doesn't make anything, it just means rolling up your sleeves and getting into the trenches where the value is created with your people.

As well as being simply the right thing to do, it also helps get momentum going as the changes are visible and other people start to wonder about what is going on with this club thing. Curiosity starts to be created.

My ambition with Learning Club at BLK BOX was that people who were not originally in the club would ask to join it to create that pull. I'm happy to say that is exactly what happened. Two others had asked to join by week three.

Step 2.1: The logistics of setting up a leadership Learning Club

Now, let's look at how we structured the Learning Club.

We needed to select between six and ten people from the senior team – directors, managers, supervisors, and/or influencers who would be taking part.

- We would have a kick-off meeting with the team to deliver clarity for all on the objectives and methodology that we were adopting.
- Everyone needed to read or listen to the *2 Second Lean* book over a four-week period. Here is the app I

was telling you about that can help with that: https://paulakers.net/lean-play
- Create a WhatsApp group for sharing learning and improvements.
- Each Friday afternoon, we would hold two-to-three-hour Learning Club meetings to discuss that section of the book and show improvements individuals made. We would generally look at a couple of supplementary videos on the key points but certainly not death by PowerPoint.

This would not just be classroom-based but going into the workplace to learn to see waste and get working on it.

Step 2.2: Learning Club content

The three big concepts we focused on in the Learning Club were:

- Building a lean culture is about pull, not push. Improvement starts with "I".
- Lean is about growing and developing people.
- Lean Done Right is about repetition and total participation.

We used the *2 Second Lean* book as the backbone for the Learning Club, discussing the content each week. The additional key content, especially regarding what the internal coaches needed to do, is outlined in Section 2.4.

Step 2.3: Establish a "Lean Cave"

During this time, I had become friendly with Alex Ramirez (from the Candour chapter!), through the amazing "Lean Maniacs" Signal group run by Dave Lelonek of Sticky RX.

Dave Lelonek of Sticky RX https://youtu.be/ZRPmhFNocGA

Can't find anything to improve? BS

Dave Lelonek

(This book sounds like a name-dropping pamphlet for all the best lean companies in the world, but that is how the lean community works. Some of us have never even met, especially because of COVID, but there are a fast bunch of friends who learn and grow together!). Alex had led what, in my opinion, was the best 2 Second Lean implementation in the world of 2020.

When I was embarking on the BLK BOX consultancy gig, I had consulted with Alex about the things he felt were key success factors within his strategy. In his opinion, the "Lean Cave" was one of the critical facilitation tools.

A Lean Cave is a collection of the tools and materials that people need when they start to make improvements. We make it easy for them to get going – things like Kaizen foam, knives to work with the foam, floor tape/markers, and so on. Alex's

Lean Cave is like a high-end hardware store, but for many, it can be a lot simpler than that.

Like many of the best ideas, it seems so obvious – after someone else has come up with it, that is!

Creating a Lean Cave helps create and maintain momentum. All the important tools and materials are there to make improvements right now. The team doesn't have to ask for them or wait for them to arrive. "Action this day" becomes real from the very early days of lean, and even if your company is already doing lean, I would say that it's never too late to create a Lean Cave.

Alex told me recently that people at one of the new plants implementing 2 Second Lean described the Lean Cave as being like the bottom of a Christmas tree! They would see what was there, and the tools and materials stimulated ideas as to how they could be used to make life easier. So, it works both ways: the Lean Cave facilitates improvement ideas to come into reality, but the items in the Lean Cave also stimulate new ideas!

It's so obvious when it's pointed out. Just do it!

Step 2.4: The external coach getting to know BLK BOX

For myself to play a full role, I could not just have observational knowledge; I would need to spend one to two days a week (at least a week before and during the Learning Club stage) hands-on working in the production areas and understanding what is happening in the admin/engineering areas. This was to get a proper ground-level feel of the existing culture, issues, and challenges so that I could speak from a position of experience rather than hearsay when interacting with the entire team and potentially making important change recommendations to the senior team for consideration.

Whether or not you bring in an external coach, it is super important for the "Ryan" and his senior supporters to have proper on-the-ground (on the Gemba!) knowledge about how things are ACTUALLY happening within the organisation.

Here is a personal story just to illustrate the importance of ground-level knowledge, especially for a business leader.

Before I was consciously using lean as an organisational transformation methodology, I was brought in to run a factory in France. At the time, my French was almost non-existent, and I was somewhat daunted by the prospect. There were some industrial relations issues still be resolved in the turnaround, and I'd never run a factory before, never mind in a foreign country where I didn't speak the language properly, like France!

Before taking the role, I insisted on spending two weeks on the shopfloor, building products with the guys. This had never happened before. It's not unfair to say that France's business culture can be a little stuffy, and senior people just simply didn't do things like this. I know that most of the middle management team that would be reporting to me thought I was a crazy Irish man. In many ways, I wouldn't argue with that analysis...

My initial briefing from the London-based board/ownership team was that "France" had a very difficult bunch of people working there – typical "lazy French" with bad attitudes. That was the problem. They would love to have closed the facility down and moved it to eastern Europe for cost-savings, but due to those pesky frogs' labour regulations, that would have cost a fortune, so they just had to put up with it.

Anyhow, my two weeks were HIGHLY illuminating! I discovered an absolutely amazing bunch of people who just wanted to turn up to work, do a good job that they could be proud of, be shown some respect, and go home. I've since discovered that this is true for every single nationality on the planet. **Lean never "goes wrong" because of the shopfloor, ever! It only ever goes wrong because of crappy management and lack of leadership.** Please don't forget that!

The Olaer building (now Parker) in Colombes, a suburb of Paris where I learnt "on the Gemba"

The real problem was at the middle management level; they basically all hated each other, and therefore, the different departments struggled to work together cohesively. The previous production manager hated the technical manager, who hated the quality manager, who, in turn, hated the production and technical managers. As they say in France, it was a *"bordelle"* or a *"connerie"*! You can look those words up if you like. The answers aren't pleasant. Sales were under a different director, and those guys just had to put up with the bad performance.

We were already bringing a stellar production manager in my friend Nic Jameron, and it didn't take long to move out the quality and technical managers and replace them with better. Change the people or change the people.

Myself & Nic representing the French & Irish nations!

The thing is, without my time on the Gemba, it might have taken me a lot longer to realise what the real trouble was. Without on-the-ground knowledge, I could still have been working under the assumption that the problem was in the shop.

As a leader, you need to work from knowledge, not assumptions. You can't coach people if you don't understand the environment. Never be too good to go on the Gemba and get your hands dirty. Taiichi Ohno had a famous practise called "Ohno's circle", where he would chalk out a circle on the floor and instruct the manager to stay there for hours while he observed the process. Real first-hand information. Not data. Not a report. Real observed data. Go to the problem, don't try to solve it from your desk!

I was "out of France" within 18 months, and under the amazing stewardship of Nic and the late Mr Christian Lecossier, it eventually went on to become the jewel in the crown of our company, Olaer. It was our R&D centre, our centre of excellence for volume manufacture, and being in Paris didn't hurt either when it came to taking customers and important stakeholders to a place where they could be impressed. Literally for the remaining time that I spent at Olaer, going there pretty much every month was like a vacation. I loved the place and the people so much.

At BLK BOX, my Gemba time helped me to see that, like most pre-lean organisations, there were mountains of waste, some inter-departmental frictions due to personalities, and conflicting key performance indicators. Intimately learning this is absolutely key for the lead coach.

Like always, there were also some "change the people or change the people" issues that I had to surface. All very normal! All opportunities to improve through changing the culture to lean.

Step 2.4.1: Learning Club content – the detail

The target was to **build a strong team of internal coaches so that we would have a strong support organisation when we started to roll out the Morning Meetings** and Improvement Time.

We used the *2 Second Lean* book as the basis for the club, taking chunks of the content and discussing them to emphasise the key points.

There is a link & QR code to a generic version of each week's presentation included with each chapter.

Week 1 Learning Club: Introduction to "the coach" and 2 SecondLean

How we are building a LEAN CULTURE

Tom Hughes

Scan to go to presentation

https://docs.google.com/pr esentation/d/1LInP7XJFC5 rOw0hfS0RD04p-JdgIBp6 5UtbdD7z9aU8/edit?usp=s haring

When I was doing this at BLK BOX, it was very much an introduction to myself, my own lean journey, and what lean is and is not, together with what our roadmap looked like over the coming weeks.

I made a big point about how I used to perceive lean vs what I actually now know lean to be. Pull not push, growing people, and repetition and total participation.

This is particularly useful to get in early because many people in our organisations have bad experiences of "corporate lean" from other places where they have worked, especially larger ones. We certainly had this issue at BLK BOX. This leads people to a place of complacency and, in some cases, of arrogance with an "I know what lean is" attitude. We need to knock that on the head straight away. Whatever the TIMWOODS (an acronym consultants use to help people memorise the eight wastes) you might have learnt in your last place, unless it had total participation, this is completely different. We're all doing this. Every day. Not the traditional top few.

Our focus is on engagement, not the key performance indicators and flipcharts and dry workshops. It's not about everyone else improving; it's all about YOU improving and leading by example.

This early introduction covered the basic "system" of 2 Second Lean, with:

- The Morning Meeting, where we build culture and learn to see waste together. We use it to set expectations for everyone. We all need to make one 2-Second improvement every day.
- 3S (sweep, sort, standardise) Improvement Time, where we all have the opportunity to apply our learning in our workplaces and processes and posting our improvements in our WhatsApp group.
- Reinforce the expectation in the Morning Meeting the following day by celebrating our improvements and deepening our understanding of waste to keep the improvement cycle going.

It's a cycle. It's a process, and because it's a process, we should always look at how it can be improved!

Learning Club
Chapters 1 - 6

Tom Hughes

https://docs.google.com/p resentation/d/1KP1yGPn PhT1CJZzLF4UeZGJ7S Ea0jLXmtZ3tSv5yBI4/edit ?usp=sharing

Scan to go to presentation

We begin by reviewing the three big concepts: pull not push, growing people, and repetition and total participation. This isn't an accident. I want the guys to experience that. I want them to ask themselves, "Why are we doing this again?" Then it's funny when I test them who remembers and to see how few of them do! It's much better to learn through doing than just by seeing and listening.

Then we discuss the chapters one by one as a group. A lot of the key principles show themselves in the early stages of the book.

I used to think that chapter 1, "What is lean?" of *2 Second Lean* was a bit of a waste of time, to be honest. At first glance, it appears that it is just setting the scene for what is to come. However, when one looks deeper, it's like the "before" of the "before and after", which is a critical concept in lean and one that we very much use to motivate each other by posting those "before and afters" in our WhatsApp groups. Done right, it really is the petrol on the fire of your lean culture.

This chapter describes Paul being happy in his ignorance. His young company is doing well: the bank loves him; in his view, he just needs to tweak a few things, like his inventory management system. It's only when Tracey delivers the "you don't know what you're doing!" line that he gets the wake-up call! The truth of the matter is that most company leaders would not listen. Why do I say that? Because "most" businesses are average, "comfortable in their dysfunction".

The leaders are either:

- Too arrogant and think they know it all, so they don't think there is a better way
- Ignorant of the fact that things can really be different
- Scared to make a big change because they are not confident in their own ability
- Aren't motivated enough to change because they just want a "lifestyle business"

That's the challenge to your company's leadership team. Where are you within this spectrum? Will you be one of the minority?

For chapters 2 and 3, "You mean I'm really that bad?" we ran a game with three teams putting a coloured sticker on a piece of A4 paper, folding it, putting it in an envelope, and writing INVOICE on the finished product and handing it to a customer.

One team of four batched each step.

Another team of four used a single piece flow.

A third "team of one" used a single operator u-shaped cell.

We ran this as a race to see which was most effective. Perhaps you can guess who finished first? Try it out and discover for yourself!

For chapter 4, "It only gets better from here", we majored on the principles of value and non-value added, with a brilliant video by Brad Cairns of Best Damned Doors fame, which illustrates this principle perfectly.

Brad Cairns Value Added vs Non-Value Added https://youtu.be/D800WMr7e_s

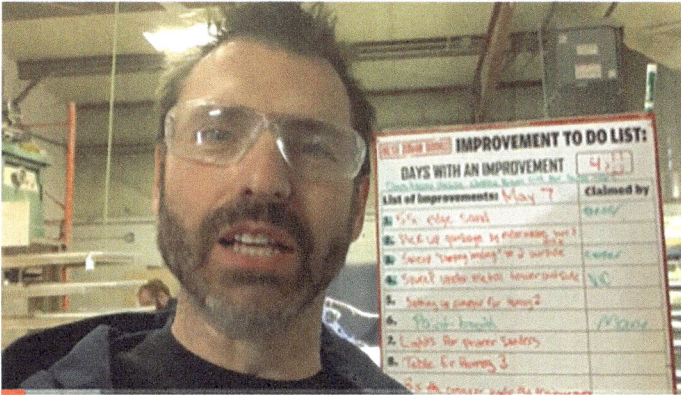

Value added V.S. No value added - Woodworking version ...

Quantum Lean

Simply put, it's only value added if there is a physical transformation or something that the customer is willing to pay for. Everything else is simply shades of waste if it's something the customer is not willing to pay for or the company would rather be doing less of it! Brad is zealous in his rigorous view of black and white waste, and while it's debatable if that is strictly correct, my personal view is that it's a lot better to start from that place than come up with all the excuses under the sun as to why your waste is okay rather than just reducing it – or better still, getting rid of it! I used other videos by Ryan Tierney and Hugh Carnahan to further deepen the understanding of this concept that I also include below.

Ryan Tierney Value Added vs Non-Value Added https://youtu.be/VWMJ0OPA0G8

Are you adding value to the customer?

Ryan Tierney

Hugh Carnahan NVA Simple https://youtu.be/Lpkmn4uFCBM

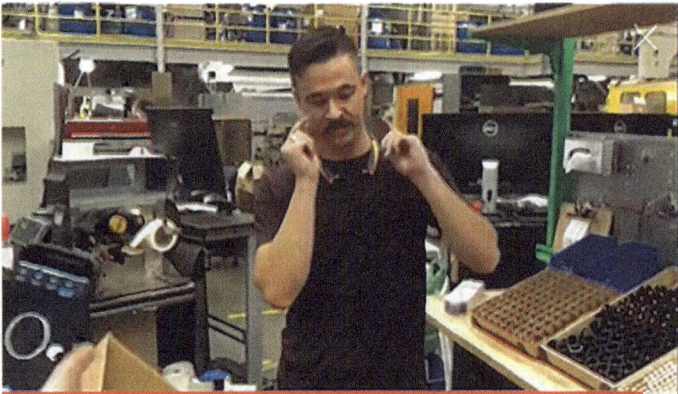

Hugh Value Add NVA SIMPLE

Tom Hughes Lumen GembaDocs Lean

For chapter 4, we also go into the eight wastes and use this opportunity to banish TIMWOOD. Many companies, especially the large ones using consultants, like to teach their people about the wastes by using acronyms.

T – Transportation
I – Inventory
M – Motion
W – Waiting
O – Over Processing
O – Over Production
D – Defects

An alternative with a similar end result is DOWNTIME.

D – Defects
O – Over Production
W – Waiting
N – Not Using Talent
T – Transportation
I – Inventory
M – Motion
E – Extra Processing

A few of these guys in our group were in the "we know lean" camp. It was fun playing a video of Mr Akers slating the use of acronyms because they do not promote UNDERSTANDING, just rote learning. There is no depth to this.

Paul Akers "How not to memorise the 8 wastes" https://youtu.be/BsItNCgbsV8

How to NOT memorize the 8 wastes

Paul Akers

Instead, we started coaching people to tell "stories about waste". Paul had done a recent podcast that was very timely on the matter. He talked about having friends over for dinner, but they weren't sure how many were coming, so they made too much salad (**Over Production** – the mother of all wastes, as you will see!). So, they had to put the leftover salad in a box (**Motion**), which was then put into the fridge (**Transportation & Excess Inventory**). After a few days, the salad didn't get used, so it went off (**Defects**), which then meant it had to go into the trash, scraping out the container (**Extra Processing**). Meanwhile, Paul's wife is **Waiting** for him to come to the sofa and give her a cuddle (**Not Using Talent** – her talent!). I ad-libbed the last piece there, but you get the picture (sorry, Leanne!). It's getting everyone to understand the story of waste and, with time, the story of waste within their own span of control, the work they do that really matters – and don't forget, acronyms suck!

Chapter 5 introduces the concept of **"fix what bugs you"**. This is one of the most powerful concepts in the book. It's the simplicity that is so beautiful: no charts, graphs, or complicated analytics. If it's annoying you, do something about it. My example where Paul helps to put on my lightbulb about struggle (see the video below) got wheeled out here for the guys. If there's a struggle or things are bunching up, you're probably not doing it right – time for an improvement!

How Paul Akers sees opportunities to improve
https://youtu.be/kB_qbOTgWvY

How Paul Akers sees opportunities for improvement

How Paul Akers sees opportunities to improve

Tom Hughes Lumen GembaDocs Lean

Chapter 6 speaks about the VP of Lexus, who gave Paul his satori method of lean being all about the people, not the processes first. Grow the people – focus on that, and the rest follows!

As you can probably imagine, this was quite an intense afternoon...

Learning Club
Chapters 7 -11

Tom Hughes

https://docs.google.co
m/presentation/d/1Mu
5-WdagNhv-k5MlBMb
NLCM-1Ah14pUlu_Vc
_S0GwWc/edit?usp=s
haring

Scan to go to
presentation

We always begin the Learning Club by reviewing all the key points from the previous week. We are not joking when we say repetition is key to learning, and it's fun seeing the penny drop with the team that just because someone has "been told" hardly ever works without repetition. This is so important to reinforce with our internal coaches, through experience, learning that "telling once/twice" rarely ever works!

You may have noted the "repetition" in the third key concept of Learning Club of "Repetition and Total Participation" and wondering what that is about. Lean is simple; however, there is a "but", and that but is that lean is also very deep.

Let's take the eight wastes. In an ordinary, traditional lean implementation, people may be subjected to a day or two of formal training around the eight wastes, IF they are lucky. Then the company plasters the notice boards and shopfloor walls with big signs proclaiming the TIMWOOD of whatever other shallow proclamation they want, and that is the "training" complete for the people. They know what the eight wastes are, right?

Wrong. They might know "of" the eight wastes but they don't "know" the eight wastes.

As you know, I love my spirituality and consider myself half Hindu, even though I'm from a farm in County Derry in Northern Ireland – hardly a hotbed of followers of the guru! I love this story about an Indian guru, Sri Yukteswar, who was asked by someone trying to test his knowledge of the scriptures. The rude protagonist asked, "Do you know the Bhagavad Gita [the Hindu Bible]?" To which Yukteswar answered, "I have read it more than a hundred times, but no, I do not know it."

That is how I see lean, and that is the attitude you need to adopt as a coach.

Putting the signs up does not mean you've trained people and certainly not that they understand it. That is done by repetition, and when done "right", *creative repetition*. It's not enough to simply put people on the spot and ask them to recite the eight wastes or even tell the story of the wastes. The training that is delivered in the Morning Meeting needs to look at the eight wastes repeatedly but from different angles. There are dozens of different ways to look at excess motion, for example, and the things that cause it. The skill of the people running the Morning Meeting is to find ways to repeat but not get boring. That can never happen.

So, on to the new stuff!

Paul's visit to HOKS and his satori moment is one of the focus areas for this week.

I am fortunate enough to be able to share my own personal experience of having visited HOKS and what a truly exceptional operation they have.

HOKS Part 1
https://youtu.be/eg80MaiGQWM

GT Tom Hoks Visit Pt 1 061119

Tom Hughes Lumen GembaDocs Lean

HOKS Part 2
https://youtu.be/LzH5lByH4Zl

"OUR FACTORY IS OUR SALES TOOL!"

HOKS Tour 061129 Pt. 2

Tom Hughes Lumen GembaDocs Lean

HOKS Part 3
https://youtu.be/ru8o-YDCHA4

HOKS TOUR part 3 061119

Tom Hughes Lumen GembaDocs Lean

To be present while all the people from that company are doing their 3S is such an inspirational experience. The level of energy they exhibit is nothing short of maniacal. Everyone gives it their all, including the owner of the $40m company, who is energetically cleaning the windows outside their reception area. They even have a team of people cleaning the street outside the factory! It's insane.

The owner at HOKS cleaning the windows: living lean culture

HOKS is the place where 5S (traditional lean) through the art of subtraction became 3S, "set in order" gets brought into standardise and "sustain," which is usually where the hardest part in traditional lean (to keep it going!) is thrown out because we don't have to worry about that with our approach as we are doing it every day!

When I teach 3S, I break it down into subgroups to help people understand what is behind each "S" and so that they can coach others.

Sweep is:

> **Clean**
> **Identify Problems**
> **Raise the Standard**

Let's talk about "**CLEAN**" first!

One of the most common misconceptions, even by people who have been "doing lean" for a long time, is viewing cleaning as a low-level activity. For them, it's like the thing people do when they aren't smart enough to come up with an improvement. Without sugar coating it, that IS sometimes the case, but it's definitely not always.

Personally, I was convinced that it's not "just pushing a broom around".

I followed up on this hunch by asking the question: "Why do we clean every day?" in the Lean Maniacs Signal group run by Dave Lelonek – in my experience, the best group in the world. I received some truly inspirational answers. Here are just some of them.

- Respect for yourself.
- Respect for others.

- Respect your work area.
- Banish sloppiness – a great work environment leads to great work.
- Minimise distractions to focus on the work.
- A clean and clear work environment is a form of visual management that reveals abnormalities and opportunities for improvement.
- Cleaning helps us raise our standards every day.
- Cleaning creates ownership of the space.
- When every single person cleans, it shows that we are all in this together.

When we boil all of these answers down, I would summarise it into three words:

CLEANING BUILDS CULTURE

So, never let anyone say, "They were just pushing a broom around". The guy who is just pushing the broom around is taking ownership of his area, respecting himself, others, and his work. He is buying into the culture. It shows that he is ENGAGED.

Your internal coaches especially need to "get this".

People "get" lean at different speeds, some straight away and some take months. I've seen guys who have been "sweepers" for months, and then they make one small improvement, the simplest thing like finding a home for the broom or the cleaning materials. When they receive some encouragement and recognition, it kindles the spark, and they "get it" some more. Keep it up, and they get to be on fire with the rest of the team.

This all requires patience, empathy, and emotional intelligence. All attributes of the lean leader. and the coach.

IDENTIFY PROBLEMS

I had a phrase that I used in my first lean transformation, **"You don't just sweep with the broom; you sweep with your head as well!"** As time goes on, we are looking for the sources of the dirt. After all, cleaning in itself is a non-value-added activity. Yes, I know, here's another dichotomy within lean, but it's true. So, we want to find ways to reduce dirt being generated, where it is coming from, and how it spreads. Most factories that I have seen are full of improvement opportunities in these areas.

When you clean the entire work area, you identify things that are anomalous. Should that "X" be there? Why is "Y" not there? This is the start of a problem-solving process which generates Improvements.

RAISE THE STANDARD

When you see the lengths that HOKS go to with cleaning, literally toothbrushing the floor to get rid of stains, you also can start to understand that cleaning is also a form of continuous improvement. When people start on their lean journeys, many are just getting rid of dirt. To quote Ryan Tierney, they used snow shovels once a week to clean the place. As the improvement effort takes hold, it's not just sweeping to the same standard as last month or year; as the regular cleaning process takes hold, people want to make it better.

"Leave it better than you found it" is such a powerful phrase. Not only does it foster respect for each other by not expecting someone else to clean up your mess, but it also asks us not to just leave it the same as we found it, but better!

When this beds into your culture and is reinforced by good coaching, it naturally leads to continuous improvement because the bar is constantly being raised.

Chapters 8 – 11 and WhatsApp exercise!

These chapters outline the bare bones of what I consider the system of 2 Second Lean, the Morning Meeting, 3S Improvement Time, and the reinforcement of behaviour with celebrating success back in the Morning Meeting from the improvements we posted in the WhatsApp group the day before.

I must say, I've never felt better in my entire career than when I was coaching improvement time in my first transformation project. The energy was incredible. I get such a kick out of watching people come out of themselves. Of course, there are the people who get it at the start, and those people never stop getting it. Each day when you as a leader/coach make your rounds, it's such a joy to see today's improvement or how they are making progress on a big improvement that is chipped away one half-hour at a time, often with guys from all different departments helping out. That is one of the surprise benefits of 2 Second Lean. Few of the larger improvement projects that emerge are done by a single person on their own; more often than not, they illicit **support from other people in the team to make it happen**. For example, someone who works on a pipe bending machine would ask the guy on the laser cutting machine to cut him a sheet of metal. He'd get help from the guy on the press brake to get it bent. Then he'd have to get a guy to weld it for him. Then it needs painting! The guy who looked after the paint shop spent most of his improvement time doing work for other people's improvements. The whole thing just greases the joints between people and different departments. **It builds teams**.

The **before and afters** are also a big part of celebrating those achievements. I describe them as the petrol on your lean fire. It's critical that your coaches constantly celebrate and encourage.

So far in the Learning Club, we had some engagement in the WhatsApp group – the usual early adopters posting their stuff. It was good, but not great.

I wanted them to feel what great looked like. They'd never had an Improvement Time before or a proper Morning Meeting yet. So, I ran a little coaching experiment.

"Right, people. You each have 20 minutes to go to your personal workspace and either 3S it or make an improvement, and I need a before and after from every single one of you posted in the WhatsApp group, and we'll give a prize for the best one. Videos earn extra points over photos. Now, off you go!"

It could have been a disaster, like all these first-time experiments, but it was far from that.

I was waiting back in the meeting room, and within 15 minutes, WhatsApp was pinging like anything! Sure enough, in 20 minutes, the 12 people were back in the room, a little breathless and full of energy. The room felt amazing, but that wasn't it.

I didn't have time to "make a video" or compile what the guys had done. I hadn't even thought of that, so the in-the-moment solution was just to scroll through the media section in WhatsApp live off my laptop. So, off we went. For most people, it was their first time making a video that non-family members would see. Most guys did a voice-over and did a good-humoured job of explaining what they did, just pointing the camera at their work. Even for those, everyone was laughing, cheering, and clapping at every "after". **One big thing we noticed was how much more people engaged with videos that had someone's face in them; they definitely got the biggest cheers and by far the best reaction.**

This simple exercise was definitely the kickstart of momentum for this team. There's a great quote that captures this: **"People will forget what you say. They will forget what you did, but they will never forget how you made them feel." Maya Angelou.**

This says a lot about what real engagement is about, fostered by good coaching. As we have already discovered, real lean is not about the charts and graphs – it's about hearts and minds, in that order. Engagement is built, maintained, and grown from the hearts of the leaders to build a solid community of people who give to each other.

If your engagement is waning, it's not because you're not connecting with peoples' heads. It's because you are not connecting with peoples' hearts, and that connection ALWAYS starts with the leader having an open heart. It virtually never happens the other way round. It ALWAYS starts at the top.

I'm going to get a bit spiritual for a moment.

You can't have an open heart if you're all tense about manipulating people to do what you want them to do, or you have an energy of frustration and anger about people or things not going your way. As always, Improvement always starts with "I", and it ALWAYS starts with the leadership team giving and getting that cycle going.

I remember at one company where I was leading the transformation when I was encouraging the management team to make a lot of changes, I categorised them into the "not doing stupid ****" camp of things not to be doing. Things like giving people a hard time, really treating grown adults like naughty children when they were changing safety gloves because they were expensive, cleaning up, and decorating the works canteen not to be a totally horrible and depressing place to eat your lunch, skimping on tools and maintenance, basic things like that – not high-level stuff!

I got pushback because "you are always just wanting to give them stuff. What about them giving to us?"

Unfortunately, in my experience, it simply does not work like that. **If you want to break a cycle of behaviour or start a more virtuous one, it has to start with management making the change, and that means management opening their hearts and giving.** It also might take a little while before the return is evident; these things need to be done in the spirit of "just being the right thing to do".

My buddy Alex calls this the "circle of trust".

Management takes a move. The "shop" responds. Management takes another move. The "shop" does more. Trust spirals upwards. That's how it works.

Back to WhatsApp!

This exercise provided INSTANT recognition for the gifts of the improvement before and after pictures and videos that people made. They got to experience their colleagues laughing, smiling, and celebrating their achievements. It set things on fire! That's what happens when you get it right.

BLK BOX week 2 compilation
https://youtu.be/KWd3b-Y6cY0

Awesome BLK BOX week 2 compilation

Tom Hughes Lumen GembaDocs Lean

BLK BOX best of week 1 videos https:// youtu.be/lu9y06L7nic

BLK BOX best of week 1 videos

Tom Hughes Lumen GembaDocs Lean

BLK BOX: amazing energy and Learning Club clip https://youtu.be/QjeJpBcZNAs

BLK BOX ENERGY AND LEARNING CLUB

Tom Hughes Lumen GembaDocs Lean

I often think that people can rarely put themselves in the shoes of another. It's especially important as a coach.

Think about it. You are a new starter or a junior member of staff, and you go to the Morning Meeting. These "big" people tell you that they want you to make improvements and post in the company WhatsApp group. So, after a week or two, you get the courage to make a post. It took guts for you to do that. You make the post, and the reaction is?... tumbleweed. No one thanks you. How would YOU feel about that?

How about if you made another improvement, another video, even after you received zero recognition for the first one? How would you feel then?

This stuff is not rocket science!

So, the lesson we need to hear in this instance that 100% needs to be built into your 2 Second Lean routine is where you will make sure that **every single improvement contribution is recognised and that the really "above and beyond" contributions are truly full-on celebrated.**

That team from Learning Club are core in driving things forward in these early weeks. They were going to be the first leaders of the Morning Meetings and, just as importantly, were going to be the 12 apostles for lean! We made it clear that they were the ones who were going to need to build momentum in the WhatsApp group, **setting the tone by making improvements themselves and coaching their respective teams to get going with their improvement efforts.**

Week 4 Learning Club

Learning Club

Tom Hughes

https://docs.google.co
m/presentation/d/1Hw
zXRo9wTTp77QVfpG
JbWRE3IzAaGR2VM
PRnMKaW2lc/edit?us
p=sharing

Scan to go to
presentation

Here is a really important slide that we covered during this week to set behaviour expectations of our coaches.

Triple X leadership

We have touched on triple X in the Candour chapter, but we will go into it in more depth here.

The first point is super important: the more senior the person, the more important it is to take it on board. Triple X stands for extraordinary, exceptional example.

Paul Akers "Triple X Leadership"
https://youtu.be/nAOETYLhB7M

The Key to Lean

Paul Akers

Our Learning Club coaches must exhibit triple X by taking the lead. Making the improvements, coaching the team, and posting to the WhatsApp group every day at least once, and they need to encourage their people.

The triple X leader always shows appreciation for other people's efforts. They thank people face to face and on WhatsApp, they celebrate them in the Morning Meeting, and they get excited about other people's improvements.

I'm lucky that I naturally get really excited by the smallest improvement people in the team make. Some of the ones that have touched me personally would not seem that great to someone else. Things like the first improvement that someone with very poor English who has been super quiet makes, like mounting a broom on his workstation. It might not be a rocket-science Instagram improvement, but it shows that this person is engaging. It shows that he wants to get involved and do better. **To say it again: at these early stages, the improvements don't matter – engaging people does!**

Another skill that the lean leader/internal coach needs to develop is the **"art of deflection".** This is not like a normal corporate BS world, where everyone tries to take credit for everything regardless of whether they did it or not! I had an old boss who used to say, "Success has many fathers, but failure is an orphan". In another toxic organisation, someone actually presented my department's improvement work and results as their own, not realising that I was in the room! In a lean company, especially as a triple X leader, it's the opposite of that. Try to give the credit to others and take less of the credit yourself. I'm not saying to lie but **be magnanimous about how credit is distributed.** Deflect it if possible on to someone else in the wider team, especially to newer, less senior members.

Now, all of that is a high bar, but why allow that bar to be any lower? This is such an important point for leader coaches to understand. Lean only ever fails because the leaders are not consistently triple X, coming-from-the-heart and therefore not getting the engagement that it all stems from.

If your lean process is having problems, the first place to look as leader coaches is in the mirror.

Don't say no – support, encourage, listen

You might notice the line "DON'T SAY NO!" That is so important, especially in the early days of 2 Second Lean. I've seen awful leaders pour cold water on the embryonic ideas of a team member, and it's one of the fastest ways to kill your lean culture. Unless someone's idea will negatively impact safety or quality or incur a big expenditure that is more than likely going to be a waste, encourage everyone's ideas. Even if you, as a coach, have a much better idea!

The most important thing, especially in the early days, is that everyone's ideas are welcomed and as far as possible, taken on board. I've watched so-called leaders "um" and "ah" when a team member is being an enthusiastic puppy full of improvement ideas, only to have their good energy dashed because it's not quite perfect – or more importantly, not perfect enough in the leader's eyes. So, yes, two of the other lines on the slide build on this point: **"mistakes will happen"** and **"growing people is more important than improvements".** Engagement and building it is the main objective. With skilful nurturing, improvements will always follow. It's a marathon, not a sprint.

Keep to your own individual span of control

Another common issue when an organisation starts on the road of 2 Second Lean is that some people want everyone else to improve – apart from them. So, when a coach makes their rounds on the Gemba during Improvement Time, which is one of their most important tasks, is that they receive improvement suggestions like, "Hey, why don't we change the ERP system [Enterprise Resource Planning system that the entire company is run on] and then my life would be easier?" "Why don't we buy a new XYZ multi-million-dollar thing, then everything would be better?" One important task of the coach is to bring the individual's attention down to their own span of control. Fix What Bugs YOU and what you have the power right now to change. That is what our expectation is, and bring them back to that. It's not that we won't fix or change the big stuff; it's just that that is not where the focus is right now. Let's get the team to show what great improvements we can make right now, and as we do that more and more, the company will get more confidence to back bigger changes and make more investments to make improvements happen.

NOW IT WAS TIME TO GET GOING!

With our BLK BOX Learning Club, this was the last weekly session before we would get going with lean "proper" – and this meant starting the Morning Meetings.

We continued with Learning Club for another three weeks. The content of which shall now be discussed in the concluding chapter, Consistency.

TAKEAWAYS

- **All truly great lean organisations have great coaches at their head.**

- Coaching is best learnt by doing.

- A Learning Club provides a great platform to grow your internal coaches and set expectations.

- **Lean never goes wrong on the shopfloor. It's ALWAYS a leadership problem.**

CHAPTER 4

The Fourth "C" – CONSISTENCY

**"Success is neither magical nor mysterious.
Success is the natural consequence of
consistently applying basic fundamentals."**
— E. James Rohn

There are so many "ke" words that I could have chosen for this chapter! Kata ("routine" in Japanese), Kaizen (small steps of continuous improvement), and Continuous Improvement as a term in itself, but I settled for Consistency.

I chose that word deliberately because it's not very glamorous. Consistency could sound like the boring part of the "lean recipe", the rinse and repeat part, but it cannot be left out, and providing the other Cs are being dealt with, it's where the Engagement is built, Improvement happens, and Results are delivered.

Consistency in this sense is about putting one foot in front of the other.

I climbed Kilimanjaro in 2014, and it was by far the toughest physical challenge I've ever taken on. We hiked for 12+ hours a day for five days, never got more than a few hours' sleep every night due to the freezing temperatures, and I had to wear the same basic clothes for the last couple of days due to my gear getting wet with no way of drying it. It was HARD!

Heading up Kilmanjaro with Mike Blenkinsop and Mike Kay, my good friends from Olaer

On summit morning, we had to get up at 3 am in the dark and hike up to the top to be there in time for sunrise. It was also by far the coldest temperatures we had to hike in because it was the middle of the night and the highest altitude. The water froze in my drinking bottle inside my backpack because it was SO COLD. I was absolutely exhausted due to the lack of sleep and the previous five days' exertions. It was a pretty miserable period, I can tell you.

The only thing that got me through it was literally the concept of "one step at a time".

I didn't worry about the next four or five hours of effort it would take to get to the top. I just focused on taking each single, individual step. That wasn't too hard. Anything beyond that, and it would have seemed insurmountable. It could have made me give up. So, no, I just took one step at a time, and I made it!

My Houston buddy, Alex Ramirez inadvertently provided me with some similar inspiration while he was playing tennis against someone much younger and fitter than him. When they first started playing each other, he was always losing. He was always looking for the fancy killer shot to catch his adversary off guard. However, as soon as he just started simply focusing on getting the ball over the net, just being simple and consistent, he started to win all the time. In Alex's words, **"You don't need to be a hero; just do the simple stuff CONSISTENTLY".**

That's what this Consistency chapter is about: building up a consistent routine that constantly evolves but never gets missed within your organisation that works for you. That Consistency is built from basic fundamentals when you apply lean.

The first fundamental is the Morning Meeting, which will drive your whole lean culture change and keep it going for years! It cannot be viewed as just an everyday, half the people turn up, boring, paint-by-numbers session that many regular internal company meetings are.

It must be different.

I use the term "domino effect" to describe just how big an impact the Morning Meeting can have when done properly.

The Domino Effect (Morning Meeting for us!) https://youtu.be/YXn08b5IIlo

Domino Effect

The Alignment Group

The domino effect states that when you make a change to one behaviour, it will activate a chain reaction and cause a shift in related behaviours too. In the words of Stanford professor BJ Fogg, "You can never change just one behaviour. Our behaviours are interconnected, so when you change one behaviour, other behaviours also shift".

Your Morning Meeting is comparable to the domino effect because it is the one opportunity that the company leadership will have to **set the tone** (excellence!), align people, and motivate everyone to improve and engage with their work, colleagues, and organisation. **Treat the Morning Meeting casually, treat your culture casually.**

I told the guys at BLK BOX to treat preparing their MM in the same way they would prepare for a presentation to a key client. It's just as important to get that right. We want everyone to look forward to the Morning Meeting as an energising experience, to build that culture, grow those people, learn to see waste, and celebrate success together!

Nico leading one of the first Morning Meetings at BLK BOX

One of the questions that Greg (the BLK BOX Managing Director) posed to me was whether we should start off lean in "an area", like production. It's a good question, and like most good answers, it begins with, "It depends". When I once prepared the approach for the 1000 people concrete company, we were going to pick a business unit area of one hundred-odd people and build a "centre of excellence" for lean. The idea was that we would do a fantastic job in one area and build that all-important curiosity so that the other units would want to do it too. Pull, not push.

However, for an organisation of BLK BOX's size of less than 100 people, I was very much against that approach.

Lean has a bad enough rap about being only a thing for manufacturing that this would have sent all the wrong messages.

If you're going to do 2 Second Lean and you have less than 100 people, then one single Morning Meeting is the way to go.

Another common question is: "do we need to do this EVERY day?"

For me, the answer is an emphatic "yes". It's about Consistency!

I don't know of a single, vibrant, lean-culture-based company that doesn't do it daily. It's about that word from the beginning of the chapter, "Consistency". **Every day we have a routine, a kata.** We don't have a "day off" from doing lean. Approaching lean like this also lets your organisation build momentum. Essentially, you're building a habit, and you don't do that with a sporadic approach. No one maintains a successful lifestyle change by doing it some days and not others.

2 Second Lean, as a model, doesn't need testing. Hundreds, if not thousands, of companies all over the world are already doing it in a successful and similar way. As the famous Toyota engagement equation says, **"Everyone, Every Day, Engaged"**. It doesn't say, "Some of the people, some days, sometimes engaged"!

There were almost 100 people at BLK BOX, so we already had a challenge about where to have the meeting to fit everyone in properly, then to have adequate audio-visual facilities, ensuring everyone could engage with the content. In the end, we went with three big screens and a speaker system that did the job. For the first few meetings, though, they were not in place, and it was tough going as not everyone could see the content being presented. These are issues I would strongly recommend you sort before you start.

For the first week, the people leading the Morning Meeting were from the company leadership team. Even though most of these people would have been used to giving presentations, they'd not had to deliver to almost 100 people in a room for 15–20 minutes very often. It's a whole other ballgame.

With a few exceptions, we got through that first week on a mixture of adrenaline and goodwill, but overall, it went great!

I used similar advice for the people holding the Morning Meeting as I did in my first 2 Second Lean company:

- Project your voice so that people can hear you (if there is a microphone, learn how to hold it properly!).
- Always thank everyone who contributes.
- Always clap first if you want to celebrate a contribution (that gets everyone else started!).
- Finally, be an expert in your content.

That last one was an addition for BLK BOX.

Many of the guys (I include girls in that grouping!) were spending too much time just reading their slides vs engaging with their audience, using the slides as a crutch. Frankly, that is really boring. It's perfectly fine for a "newbie" or a non-leadership person to be nervous and not a television standard presenter. I'd argue that it's even a really good thing because the rest of the team connects with that person who is getting outside their comfort zone. The lack of a polished performance is actually a positive in that case because it builds team spirit. However, it's different if you're a senior figure in your organisation. You are leading. You are setting a standard. If you're super nervous because you don't know the material and are avoiding eye contact by reading off the slides, it's not good. Your nervous, negative energy will rub off on others.

No matter what, if you're a newbie or a senior figure, **rehearse and know your material because that is all part of the growth experience.** Taking the time to read up on a new angle on your education slot deepens not only your own knowledge but also that of the entire team. As per the old Latin quote, **"The best way to learn is to teach".**

The guys at BLK BOX were pretty exceptional on this point from the get-go because it was not just a single figure leading the Morning Meeting for those first days/weeks. The senior guys took turns for the first couple of weeks, then it was rolled out to the 12 apostles (internal coaches), then to others beyond that on a voluntary basis. It was super positive stuff.

Another common question people have is about the Morning Meeting agenda.

I have seen a lot of different approaches to the Morning Meeting from my own experience of lean and also on lean tours of other organisations. Most of the approaches can stem back to how Fastcap do theirs, and there are some great resources around how to do that on Paul Akers' website:

Morning Meeting Document

November 17, 2011 by Paul

Morning Meeting Document (PDF)

- 2 Second Lean
- 2 Second Lean, Lean
- < How to Shoot a Smooth Video
- > Lean in One Page / In a Nutshell

From what I've seen, however, the Morning Meeting of a six-person company can be significantly different from that of a 100-person company. The reason for that is that less than eight people can be a full-on interactive discussion, whereas when the numbers are greater than that, it is hard to facilitate that without many of the people being spectators and, in most settings, the same people who by nature are quite extroverted will tend to dominate proceedings, making things boring for the rest of the group. So, in larger organisations, the nature of communication tends to be outward – one to many rather than being heavily discursive.

This means that the Morning Meeting agenda and how it is run can be quite different depending on the organisation.

Here is a range of agenda items that can be used as a "pick 'n mix" for how you decide to run yours. I've split them into two categories, those that help you in "building culture" and those that concern education (Growing People).

Having agenda items on a rota (EVERYONE takes a turn) from day one helps foster the idea of total participation and takes some of the burden of the Morning Meeting leader. It also serves to help prepare others for taking on that mantle.

Morning Meeting Agenda Items

BUILDING CULTURE ITEMS

Stretches / Physical Ice Breaker – best on a rota with every single team member leading

Gratefuls – rota

Numbers? – choose an important KPI or two but careful not too many!

Shout outs – open

What are you proud of?

Principles – as per schedule

Quote of the day/lean quote of the day

Celebrate – video – all yesterday's improvements

Awards ceremonies

EDUCATION ITEMS

3S/eight wastes every day – on a schedule circulating through the different wastes/"S's"

3S Hero – on a rota through the entire team

Favourite improvements from other companies

Book club page – rota item through the entire team

Quality moment

Safety moment

Stretches / Physical Ice Breaker

Many find it strange that western companies are all doing stretches! Personally, while it's certainly beneficial to get peoples' energy levels up by limbering a little, the main purpose behind them is to be an ice breaker for the group. It IS an unusual activity. Not many companies are doing it, and I believe that it helps **build your organisation into its own little cult of "us!"** When you're doing them, people make eye contact and smile, and connections are being made. When you alternate the leader, you also provide an opportunity for some of the more introverted team members to express their personalities and for people to bond with them – whether they do a great job of leading them or a bad one, it's all good. I can't imagine doing a Morning Meeting without the stretches. It just would not be the same.

"Gratefuls"

The gratefuls point can seem strange, too, but fostering that attitude of being grateful for what we have is one of the cornerstones of lean. Some people use the term "givers". **Lean is about us all giving, and giving seems easier when we do it from a place of abundance.** The gratefuls helps cultivate that. Putting them on a rota with people being advised that they will be speaking tomorrow is another way to build Morning Meeting leaders. They get an opportunity to just speak a "little bit", but often, the point of gratitude has the person revealing a little of their lives outside work and expressing some vulnerability. It all builds team and grows culture.

From a recent lean tour: Daniel Lopez at Sussex Caravans doing Gratefuls & Praise

Key Performance Indicator(s)

I always stress that the Morning Meeting can never be a "production meeting", as in getting into the minutiae of what each of us has to do today. Use five to ten-minute stand up meetings for those. That is not what the Morning Meeting is about. However, it is also not isolated from reality, so those "how are we doing yesterday/this week/this month" numbers are also positive to bring into the Morning Meeting, providing an opportunity for everyone to know what the priorities are and where there might be bottlenecks that require support. The same effect can even be achieved even if it's very difficult to get good numbers to talk around. One of my corporate lean buddies tells me that at his company, they simply go around the team leaders with a "how was yesterday?" question. They all know whether they had a good day or not, so this lets them talk about positives and not-so positives from the day before and where they could do with some support. It is certainly not for beating anyone up or shaming a department. Any hard direct talking of that nature should be done outside the MM.

Shout Outs

"Shout outs" are another building culture point that should always be left open for people to randomly speak up. This is about expressing gratitude and celebrating the team member who went above and beyond help gel your team together. You can gauge how vibrant your culture is by how eagerly people are willing to shout out their colleagues' support.

What are you proud of?

"What are you proud of?" is an agenda item done at Seating Matters to build engagement. According to Ryan Tierney, everyone has SOMETHING they are proud of and they want to tell people about. This is especially good when it has absolutely nothing to do with the workplace, as it demonstrates people giving of themselves to the team when they share.

Last time I participated in the Morning Meeting at Seating Matters, the lady holding the meeting presented a photo of her with her grandchildren, telling everyone how much joy she got from being around them and how proud she was of them. It was so heart-warming.

It is this opening up and revealing their real, non-work team member selves that is the real fuel in your engagement locker. It's far from just engaging with management; it's about engaging with the team at multiple levels. This builds trust, engagement, and commitment to the cause.

Lean Principles

This is an agenda point that I used "with an agenda" during my first 2SL implementation. We had so many problems with culture around lack of mutual respect and blaming people when things went wrong. **I developed the company lean principles as I encountered different cultural problems to get the ownership team and the wider team to face them and adopt another approach.** I used principles like "no BMW" to inject humour into serious subjects. I'd ask who knew what BMW stood for. I'd get all kinds of car-related answers, ranging from the humorous to the serious. My "reveal" would be Blaming, Moaning, and Whining. I don't want to hear any of that around here anymore, and we'd get a few laughs. Another one to advance change on this similar topic was "Attack the _____, not the _____". Ask for guesses as to what the blanks represented and then do a reveal, "Attack the process, not the person". I'd repeat the new point for a few days before moving on to a new one, and when I had developed 21 in total, I put that on a daily repeat rota that we would cycle over day after day to deepen it further into our culture.

Quote of the Day

I used to use this item with a similar agenda. I was not just looking for pretty-sounding few words; I generally wanted to convey a serious message behind the quote I used. Lean quotes from the founding fathers of lean are also brilliant as education tools. Finding a quote can also be a task that the person chairing the Morning Meeting can have as part of their preparation as your culture becomes more mature. Depending on the number of people in your meeting, you can choose whether this part of your meeting is an opportunity to discuss the concept behind the quote in more depth.

Celebrate Success

This is an essential piece of culture-building that the best lean organisations do at the end of their Morning Meeting. At the very least, show the best of yesterday's improvements from the team.

The best practise is to put every single before and after and at least a clip of each improvement video into a less than a four-minute video at the end of the Morning Meeting to finish it on a motivational high. People love to see "their bit", and it's best if the voice-over narrative shouts people out by name. When I first started putting YouTube improvement videos and compilations of them into the WhatsApp group of the original company where I did 2 Second Lean, I found out through the backdoor that people were sharing them with friends and family, a bit like as we say in Ireland, "Being on the telly!" I love this kind of recognition and the feeling of appreciation this generates.

Tom Hughes "Recognition: the key to success" https://youtu.be/IFjWtif8UEk

Recognition : the key to engagement

Tom Hughes Lumen GembaDocs Lean

Often, these guys have never had the words "thank you" said to them with regards to work, and now, someone is making crazy cool videos and bigging them up in front of the company and, in some cases, with lean videos that are seen by thousands of people all over the world in the lean community. What is not to like about this? Showing that video at the end of the meeting sets the tone for the team to go out and do it all over again!

Recognition Awards

Nobody would normally associate lean with the Oscars, but I've seen the connection in action. I came up with the idea while working with the guys at BLK BOX. They were making their celebration videos every day, but I thought there could be more. I came up with the idea of an awards ceremony to put recognition on steroids. We told the team that there would be awards for Best Improvement, Best Video, Best Before & After, Best Team, and Outstanding Contribution. I'm not sure they really knew what I meant by the B-BRAs (BLK BOX Recognition Awards).

On that Friday morning, I came in dressed in a tuxedo with black tie. At the entrance to the Morning Meeting, we played typical awards ceremony music, and I tee'd up people to present the awards, complete with envelopes containing the nominations and winners. It was great fun. I know I was probably considered a little crazy by a lot of people, but that's half the point. If things are becoming stale, try something different and run the experiment. It might fail, but it also could be knocked out of the park. The worst thing to do is continue Einstein's definition of insanity, doing the same thing over and over again and expecting different results.

In the same vein, some companies (Seating Matters springs to mind) invite external speakers in to spice the meeting up and present a new angle on an education topic – health and fitness, for example, where they got a top trainer to come in and show some new stretches and deliver talks on nutrition and exercise.

Ultimately, the cardinal sin is to let the Morning Meeting get stale. Do whatever you must to stop that happening at all costs.

EDUCATION ITEMS

The "Education" segment is where the "content" is. This is the main part towards achieving our growing people agenda, or learning to see waste.

There is a plethora of information available, especially on YouTube, that provides great material for training your people. Sometimes it can seem to take an eternity to dig it out at the start of your journey, but it gets easier.

3S/Eight wastes every day – on a schedule circulating through the different wastes/"S's"

At the beginning, it makes sense to spend a few MMs consecutively on each waste or "S" of the 3Ss, so people don't get the feeling that they are skimming over the subject in too superficial a way. Then, after that initial foundation has been laid, get going with putting that on a daily schedule, rotating through the eight wastes and 3S on a daily basis.

That repetition never stops, but as you progress, other education points can be added, different lean tools (e.g., Kanban or Kamichibai Boards), product training, competitor benchmarking on a particular aspect, or an industry trend/development. As long as it serves your people to help deepen their knowledge and stimulate improvements, it's all good. It's really important that your repetition does not get stale, however. **Boring is not what we are after. I coined a term called "creative repetition"** to put this point across. Yes, we want to deepen our understanding of the eight wastes and 3S, but we need to make sure that we look at each individual waste from a variety of different angles rather than the same thing over and over. At the same time, it's perfectly fine to repeat a brilliant piece of material a few times to make sure that the learning gets in there. It really just requires good judgement to find a balance.

It's great to get your education from the people within your team. There will always be some people who get lean at a higher level much faster than others, so it's great to use those leaders as examples to educate and inspire others within the team.

3S Hero – on a rota through the entire team

I used to do the "3S Hero" slot in my first organisation on a rota, where each team member had to do a video of their workplace, how they had 3S'd it, and recite the 3Ss the way that we were teaching them. Some of the guys' English was really poor, so we allowed them to do it in their own language with the help of a colleague to translate. This is another example where an obstacle can be turned into an opportunity; getting people to help each other out and get out of their comfort zone while showing off their learning to others and having the opportunity to collectively learn is again just the juice that gets lean flowing.

"Favourite Improvement from other companies"

This is one that Seating Matters do every day. Like myself, the guys at Seating Matters are members of various WhatsApp and Signal groups where dozens of improvements from different companies are shared. The ones that resonate with them are shared with their team to simulate their minds about how those innovations might be applied within their work environments.

Quality/Safety Moment

We used to have an agenda item, "Defects", in my first company, but this term comes with a lot of finger pointing! I've seen it much better done with "Quality Moment". This agenda item can be used to highlight a recent defect that occurred internally or reached a customer, informing the team and communicating on what countermeasures have taken place to prevent re-occurrence. A similar approach can be used for Safety Moments to highlight near misses, accidents, or any new policies or processes around safety improvement.

But you can (and kinda must!) do your own thing with your Morning Meeting and Improvement Time!

These are just some agenda items that may get your creative juices flowing, but it's likely you will develop your own style and agenda items that **will work best for your organisation.** The key is Consistency, never miss the Morning Meeting, and keep these meetings filled with positive energy. It's about constantly deepening the understanding of your people around the culture and wastes so that the improvements and consequential results come!

Sitting alongside the Morning Meeting is the second fundamental of "3S Improvement Time", which is when the team gets the opportunity to put their learning into practise by applying it to making improvements, reducing the struggle and waste in everything we do. As we've touched on earlier, most companies take half an hour for this. This is enough time for most organisations to allow for a good clean up and improvements to be made.

From a leadership perspective, the most important point I can make here is being visibly interested and "Triple X" for your team with Consistency. **If you scurry back to your desk after the Morning Meeting, you send out all the wrong signals.** If you are only visibly present "the odd time", it sends out the same non-Consistent, no-Commitment message. The entire organisation needs to be on the Gemba, ESPECIALLY the leadership team. No excuses. All the time.

The Morning Meeting and Improvement Time combined are your "kata". This is a Japanese martial arts term that best matches our English word, "routine". A good lean process is based on a clear kata and the most important one, if you want to be truly great, is the one you do daily with Consistency.

Continuous improvement of "how you do Lean" – PDCA/PDR/Hansei

A key part of your lean system needs to be creating a feedback loop on your overall process and how it is going. PDCA stands for Plan Do Check Action and is often called the "Deming Cycle" after its creator WE Deming. PDR or Plan Do Review is a similar variant of the same process.

PDCA Cycle
https://youtu.be/RrWW4wDYf2k

PDCA Cycle

Plan
Do
Check
Act

Plan
Do
Check
Adjust

PDCA Cycle | Plan Do Check Act | Deming Cycle

LeanVlog

If Taiichi Ohno is the "Father Of Lean", Deming could be called the "Grandfather" because he was a leader of the original group of American engineers who brought these principles to Japan after WWII. Fundamentally, it's about being deliberate that the quality of your process inputs are constantly reviewed to ensure the process is kept stable and produces high-quality results.

The second part I recommend is more of an attitude rather than a system: "Hansei."

This Japanese word has various meanings depending on the definition you use, but the overall meaning I choose to coach is to "look back with regret". I first learnt about the principle in Japan on my lean study mission.

We had an amazing visit to a Japanese primary school at lunchtime. There were about 500 kids having lunch in this canteen, happy as anything, smiling and talking with each other. In spite of that, our group could still converse with each other without raising our voices! The kids went up and collected their trays of healthy food, already telling the server that if there was anything they did not think they would eat to minimise any wasted food.

When they were finished with their meals, they put all the materials in the right recyclable waste containers, and there was hardly any waste! Quite a lot different to things in the West. When they were leaving the dining room, each child went up individually to say thank you to the kitchen staff who had prepared their meal and next, you won't believe what they were going to do.

The next part of lunchtime was about the entire school cleaning it! The schools don't have janitors over there – the kids do everything themselves: vacuuming and polishing floors and windows, weeding the lawns and flower beds, even taking the old leaves out from underneath bushes! The energy was incredible, and it was really clear from their attitudes that they were happy to do this. They were happy and smiling, having fun; it wasn't like watching forced labour! However, I still have not got to the most impressive part!

At the end of cleaning time, each class got together for their hansei. There is no official leader. The kids say things like, "I wasn't really on form today, I was just messing around. Sorry for that. I will do better tomorrow!" Not everyone, just a few, and it wasn't a shaming exercise. The other kids would be giving back an attitude of "that's okay, thanks for telling us; we will do better tomorrow". It was just amazing for me to witness. I was so impressed.

The level of maturity these kids exhibited was just jaw-dropping. They were only nine years old...

When I was coaching with BLK BOX, I explained to the guys that regularly **"looking back with regret"** was a great practise and spirit to cultivate. I encouraged them to ask, "How did I do?" after the Morning Meeting they had led, with a spirit that went beyond, "Great, mate!" but actively want constructive criticism as to how we could do it better next time, either as an individual or as a team.

Each week on Friday afternoon, we did a "Hansei" to reflect on the "things gone well" and the "things gone not so well" from the previous week, looking at various ways that we could improve that all-important engagement. I discovered years ago that there is a whole different flavour to using those terms rather than the traditional "things gone wrong/things gone right" approach. It encourages more honesty and less blame within the team and gets the creative juices flowing. We are all learning together.

We came up with a proxy metric for our engagement to ascertain how we were doing. This was to count how many media posts we were getting in our WhatsApp group and use them as an indicator for how many improvements we were making and what the level of engagement was.

We also compiled a league table of the people and departments who were making the most improvements and had the highest level of engagement. These numbers were also communicated to everyone in the Morning Meeting. The idea is to pull others along and provide extra recognition for those going above and beyond.

BLK BOX, being a sports fitness company with a strong culture associated with that, had a group of people who loved competing. So, in a positive way, being top of the league became something that departments and individuals strove for. It put a smile on peoples' faces. It was fun, and while this might not work in every company, **the key is to find what is fun to YOUR people**, builds team, and drives engagement consistently.

Developing these daily, weekly, and monthly milestone checks within your kata and applying them with Consistency is so important to make sure that your efforts don't start drifting off the rails, which they certainly will. No one said this was easy. Those trials are part of your team's development opportunities when doing 2 Second Lean. If/when people stop seeing more waste or don't know where the next improvement is coming from, that is a sign, an opportunity to grow. It requires Commitment and means that you need to dig deeper to bring more training and education to your team so that they can see the waste or spot that next improvement.

That is where your team will find the biggest and best parts of 2 Second Lean, providing they don't take the easy route and blame the system. It's not the system; it's their depth of understanding that is lacking.

The Four Ps: Priority, Practise, Patience, Persistence

I was really fortunate at this stage of my BLK BOX coaching in that I came across a social media post from a guitar tutor friend of mine talking about how to learn to play the guitar. He spoke about practise, persistence, and patience. I thought it had great cross-over potential to doing lean. You need to do it regularly, and by that, we mean every day – practise. You need to keep at it, even when you don't feel like it (persistence), and lastly, the results are unlikely to come in a day or two; it takes time before you see evidence of success (patience). In spite of lean being the "art of subtraction", I added another "P" to it: priority.

None of that happens if you don't make lean a priority. It's actually more important than any of these, as without it, none of the rest has a chance.

To illustrate this, I will use the example of my own guitar playing.

Tom Hughes "The Power of the 4 Ps and 3X" https://youtu.be/huNed633Ua8

The power of 4Ps and 3X

Tom Hughes Lumen GembaDocs Lean

When I was a kid, I had a guitar, and I learnt about a dozen chords, but because I was a good singer and used to play in bands that way, I never felt motivated to learn to play the guitar at a good level. For my 40th birthday, I spent about $1000 on a nice Takamine guitar because I thought now was the time to put more effort into learning how to play. I did for a few weeks and then stopped. I still couldn't play any tune properly, despite that I knew the chords, I knew what to do – as in "how" to play the guitar intellectually – but I'd never made it a **priority** to put in the time to **practise** necessary to become a good guitar player, or had the **patience** and **persistence** to get those results. The priority was the problem. The rest I can do for other things, like meditation, for example. I haven't missed a morning meditation in over three years. My meditation practise is the foundation that the rest of my life is built on, and I derive tremendous benefits from it. At the time of writing, I'm now learning to become a high-level meditation teacher, and I'm very comfortable to be able to come from a place of strong experience to do so. The only difference between meditation and the guitar? Priority.

I was recently talking with another senior corporate lean buddy about this stuff, who is now helping other divisions and units within his massive organisation to apply 2 Second Lean. However, the mentality of a "typical" corporate mindset can be a huge barrier. Everyone is so focused on their KPIs (and only the KPI's!), delivering their short term results up the chain, and I can categorically say that if that is your focus and emphasis when trying to apply lean, then your efforts will be short-lived. In real cultural transformation, results are often the last thing that becomes evident.

The focus ALWAYS has to be around engagement. That's about wholehearted buy-in from everyone: total participation. This is especially important at the beginning of your lean journey.

If it's about getting results, your people will smell your lack of authenticity about this just being another "tool", you will not get engagement, and you will fail on your journey before you even really started. So, it's all about engagement, engagement, engagement.

When you get engagement, which can be measured in smiles and body language, the next thing you will see are improvements as people jump on the train in their own time. Each person's individual level of understanding develops at their own personal pace as they "get it". Pull with only a little push.

Grow the people, build the culture, and the rest will follow.

Push is reserved only for people actively stopping the process from moving forward, destructively resisting it. Two words apply to them, with zero tolerance: get out!

As the improvements gather steam, you will start to see the results improving. It can take a few months. Generally, physical transformation of the workplace happens in weeks, and real tangible improvements start to trickle out over the first weeks but months to really get momentum, then the results start to take off and keep going off the chart as your kata develops consistency and momentum.

That only takes place with priority, practise, persistence and patience or, alternatively put, Candour, Commitment, Coaching and Consistency. It's all a matter of leadership, human behaviour, and not a little bit of love – a little-used word in business circles.

All challenges are opportunities to grow

True lean is not felt in the head; it is felt in the heart. It is a heart-based exchange between souls. If your lean journey is ever going in a direction you don't like, look in the mirror as a leader to discover where you are going wrong. Then open your heart to your people in a spirit of understanding to know what needs changing. Often, it will be you that needs to change. Sometimes they will realise that they need to change, and other times, as a leader, you will need to change the people or change the people. No matter what happens, every obstacle is an opportunity for growth. Every interaction, every challenge starts with "I".

The real learning is not done during the easy times; it happens when things are tough. The learning doesn't occur when someone else solves the problem for you; it only truly happens when you search for your own solutions by digging deeper and finding ways to make things work.

There is an Indian parable about the caterpillar struggling to get out of the cocoon. It can struggle for an entire day to push itself out, and when it succeeds, it becomes a beautiful butterfly. A "kind" human could look at the poor caterpillar struggling and "help" it by cutting away the cocoon to set it free. However, that kind of kindness can kill. The butterfly needs to struggle out of the cocoon, squeezing the moisture out of its wings so that it can fly. Without the struggle, that doesn't happen, and it withers and dies. **Success comes from the struggle.** While shortcuts exist, they may not do good in the long run. You need to find your own way through.

It calls to mind one of my favourite lean quotes from Mr Amezawa, whom I had the pleasure to meet during my study mission with Paul Akers.

"Be happy when you have problems. They are opportunities to grow."

Me with Mr Amesawa – a real gentleman of wisdom

You will ALWAYS have challenges in life. It's designed that way. You can waste your energy trying to "resist what is", pulling yourself into stress, anxiety, and drama, OR you can consciously relax, open your heart, and ask, "What am I supposed to be learning from this?", embracing your challenges in whatever form they take and see how it goes.

You always have a choice as to which approach you take, but I can promise you that embracing this attitude will lead you down a much better road than the widespread current practise of blaming the world for your problems.

It all works much better when you realise that "Improvement starts with I".

- **Build your own kata that happens every day: Morning Meetings and 3S/Improvement Time.**
- Morning Meetings are about engagement first, building culture and growing people through education.
- Make sure you have a feedback loop to ensure that your kata never becomes stale. Positive energy is key.

CHAPTER 5

The Fifth "C" – CONTINUOUS LEARNING

"and there's more....."
— Jimmy Cricket (very cheesy
Northern Ireland Comedian)

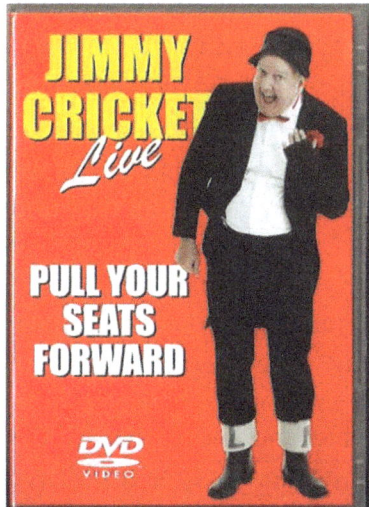

Jimmy Cricket (note the Visual Control on the boots!)

When I asked for contributions to this book from my lean friends, I expected my friend Ryan Tierney of Seating Matters to pick Commitment. I expected him to describe some huge barrier he'd had to overcome to become one of the best SME lean companies on the planet. He surprised me when he picked this chapter of Continuous Learning as his contribution.

I am not using Ryan's exact words, but here is his story.

"It all changed when I went to Japan to do the lean study mission with Paul Akers.

I made sure I sat at the seat right behind Paul so that I could pick up every little nugget of information I could and get as much from the experience as possible.

I will never forget it. JB [another amazing Seating Matters Lean Leader] was sitting beside me.

I had a total lightbulb moment.

We had just visited Mifuni, and Mr Amezawa was at the front of the bus, and he said something along the lines of, 'Toyota don't just make cars. We teach and train people'. I wrote it down in my book, and that night, I was discussing with JB and said that this was my big takeaway from this trip, and the trip had only just started!

I said, 'We are not just a company that make chairs. We are a teaching and training organisation that happen to make chairs'.

These days, we have had more than 500 people at Seating Matters for lean tours, and I say that at the beginning of every lean tour:

'We are a teaching and training organisation that happen to make chairs'.

We could make anything. We could make cars. We could make robots. It doesn't matter.

We are a teaching and training organisation that is Continuously Learning. The Morning Meeting is the most important part of our day because we are Continuously Learning.

Every single day in the Morning Meeting, we pick a different learning topic, and every single person has to take their turn holding that meeting and revising the material the night before to deepen their understanding of that topic to a level where they can teach it to others.

That all started with that lightbulb moment in Japan. Toyota is a teaching and training organisation. I thought that this is unbelievable. This is exactly what we are.

Before that, I was doing lean and making the same mistake that most other people do: I was getting caught up in the visuals. But once I understood that we were a teaching and training organisation, everything changed...."

This point is totally key to doing lean the right way. It's not about the "visuals", and certainly not the graphs and wallpaper of traditional western, corporate lean. They have their place, but they are not central to building a sustainable culture, as we have seen.

To continuously keep improving, lean organisations have to be Continuously Learning, at the level of the individual, at the level of "I" to sustain and deepen their culture.

The Morning Meeting is at the heart of that process, and everyone in the organisation needs to recognise that this is the purpose. To teach and train people.

Originally, Consistency was "almost" the end of this book, but, like all Lean Maniacs, I never stop learning. I grasped some new things while I was writing it that I just couldn't help sharing, so that's why I added this additional chapter, and it really helps illustrate this point. Learning starts with I. Lean people never, ever stop, and they have a hunger for it.

I hope you find the two final sections useful.

There are two points: "Your eight wastes may not be the same as Toyota's" and "The Importance of Standards".

Both are about strengthening your lean system but in quite different ways.

We thought we were committing "lean heresy" when we started to question the "traditional" wastes, but really, it is very strong in the tradition of the Toyota Production System to innovate your thinking and apply the system in the best way for the circumstances.

Standards are literally the foundation of lean – without them, your results will always be up to chance. So, both concepts will add value for most of you.

Now, let's go with the first!

BEYOND THE EIGHT WASTES: "YOUR EIGHT WASTES MAY NOT BE THE SAME AS TOYOTA'S"

If you watched the Lumen AME tour video from Chapter 2, you will already have an idea about what we are going to discuss here.

In my experience, without a doubt, for almost all lean companies, it has been easier to achieve and maintain momentum in the manufacturing area than it has in those that are more office-based, with computer-based, virtual processes. It's even more difficult for those organisations with significant numbers of people working remotely.

After the initial rush of adrenaline at getting started with lean, 3S'ing the office space, tidying up their PC desktops, and creating file directory structures, it is very easy for the people in those parts of the organisation to become disengaged because they simply don't know what to do next.

I've tried to help companies get over this problem by teaching that "anything the customer doesn't want to pay for" or "anything the company would rather do less of" as a way for those people to identify waste within their processes (similar to the Brad Cairns approach mentioned in the Coaching chapter), but honestly, it has a limited effect, and engaging these teams has still been a struggle.

Part of the problem is that the traditional eight wastes don't speak well to these functions, especially those who have a very limited physical dimension to their work. That's because Taiichi Ohno's seven wastes that later became eight were written for 1950's Toyota – a cash-strapped business in danger of bankruptcy. They couldn't afford to have cash tied up in inventory or in piles of half-utilised, expensive capital equipment, so the wastes he came up with were business killers for THEM, but now, those same wastes are being shoe-horned into third Millennium companies, many of whom have completely different challenges or wastes, with little or no physical product. They could hardly be more different to post-WWII Toyota.

My business partner at Lumen Electronics, Patrick Magee, was the man to spot this and have this "satori" (awakening moment) while watching Paul Akers interview lean legend Norman Bodek (RIP) during a trip in Japan. Norman described this exact issue as the reason why over 98% of American companies fail at doing lean.

We certainly had this problem at Lumen Electronics. We were able to apply the traditional eight wastes very well to our physical and especially manufacturing processes, but most of the value we create is at a computer, designing electronic circuits or writing embedded software codes. Simply put, many of the eight wastes were totally irrelevant. For example, we didn't over-produce engineering work, we didn't own a forklift, and trying to say that "inventory" was analogous to computer files costing a few dollars a month on a server is literally beyond a joke. It makes a mockery of real wastes.

Meanwhile, we certainly had real business challenges that our kaizen activities were having a limited impact upon.

So, over the space of several months, Patrick took the lead in writing **OUR eight wastes for the electronic design process that addressed OUR pain points that were causing sleepless nights for us, as well as wasting our scarce resources and causing our CUSTOMERS pain.**

Patrick used me as a soundboard, and we had some seriously robust discussions. What we were doing for many lean people was "heresy!", but after those few initial skirmishes, Patrick managed to convince me that this was the right track.

Eventually, we came up with our eight wastes, which are as follows.

Project Ambiguity: this is when it's not clear what the scope of a project is or its deliverables and leads to customer dissatisfaction because what we deliver is not what they expected, or, from our side, where we spend days working for free to give a feature or level of performance that was not planned at the outset. This is the "mother of all wastes" for this process, as when we experience this, many other wastes are multiplied, just like traditional Over Production.

Variations: where non-standard components or processes are used, which adds complexity to delivering a technical outcome or causes issues in the supply chain when launching into production.

Bad Code: code that is buggy (doesn't work well) or just as bad is difficult to comprehend by anyone but the author. This causes masses of Non-Value Added time by another engineer trying to work out the tech stack, managing that handover before they can start Adding Value (i.e., physically changing the code).

Bad Hardware: where a component doesn't behave as we had expected due to insufficient due diligence on datasheet selection or not behaving as the datasheet would lead us to believe.

Searching: for development components or code. Really a subset of traditional Over Processing, but we get real value out of calling OUR critical waste exactly what it is.

Manufacturing Integration: poor Design For Manufacture. In our case, difficult to screw together or, worse, program and test. Done badly, this costs us business.

Commercial Engagement: project proposals with inappropriate payment schedules (eating cash) or terms. Inappropriate pricing – too high or too low or not managing time spent on a project well leading to over runs.

Interruptions: "the shoulder tap" when an engineer is in deep work, headphones on writing complex code, and someone interrupts with a "where is the screwdriver for...?" type question.

We made this the key subject for our AME lean tour, and it has already resonated with hundreds of companies around the world. We are already being told about companies who are naming their "eight wastes of design" or "eight wastes of sales" and getting real value from it.

We get asked all the time, "How did you come up with YOUR eight wastes?" as other companies want to follow the same path. So, here is our recommendation.

1. The leadership team need to brainstorm the main strategic problems that are hurting the business in terms of costs, sheer frustration, or wasted opportunities.

   Initially, that should be done in a small team, with the main functional heads participating. The team members' role is to highlight the pain points within their functions, as well as those of the overall business.

   One person, preferably the most senior, should take the lead in facilitating the activity.

   Here are some potential catalysts to get the creative juices flowing for understanding what your critical wastes could be. Perhaps these are lurking in your business?

   "Bottlenecks" or "leaks" – what is stopping your business from growing faster due to a constraint, or what causes you to lose customers? All businesses have those, so name them and get them on the table for discussion with your wider team.

"Lost margin" – this could be due to inappropriate pricing to the customer, either too high (losing volume) or too low (giving the product away), which is an opportunity for the sales and finance teams to work collectively to analyse pricing strategy for effectiveness.

"Stock outs" – we talk of Excess Inventory in the traditional wastes, but the opposite is not being able to serve a customer because we have no stock. Product availability vs inventory turns can be good measures that need to be optimised together. This also provides an opportunity for sales and purchasing teams to cooperate more closely on forecasting and buying patterns/stocking policies.

"Cost of customer acquisition" – simply put, how much is it costing you to win that new customer or that new sale? Do you know? Does it make sense? Do you understand your sales funnel? Do you measure how it leaks and why?

"Non-billed work time" – perhaps a form of "Over Processing" but being explicit, especially in service-based businesses. How much of your peoples' time is billed against what you would like to bill?

"Wasted meeting time" – how much of the time spent in meetings are value-added for each individual sitting in that meeting?

"Non-value added communication" – extra emails, meetings, or phone calls, either internal or external, that did not need to happen for value to be created for the customer.

That list is not meant in any way to be exhaustive! It's just to give you some examples to get the discussion going.

They also don't need to add up to eight, by the way! It could be three, four, or five different wastes, but I wouldn't recommend having many more than eight because it will be hard to focus actions appropriately.

2. Prioritise those that are most critical and describe them in detail, in written form. When Patrick did this at Lumen, his initial paper ended up 15 pages long! You don't have to do that, but it IS important to work on delivering clarity to the rest of the team about these potential wastes.

3. Circulate the paper to all the team and meet to agree on what the list of final wastes will look like.

4. Start to make those "new wastes" part of the Morning Meeting education process.

We got a huge benefit out of NAMING THE WASTE. Rather than leaving the vague description of what waste was, as the traditional "what the customer doesn't want to pay for", being specific was like putting on a pair of waste vision goggles for our people. Once you see it, you can't unsee it, and we are now much more effective at working at reducing and eliminating them.

We reckon our wastes will also EVOLVE with time. We have already made huge strides at eliminating the waste of Project Ambiguity by having paid "discovery phases" with customers to identify the key technical issues and precisely define project deliverables at the outset, as well as taking a lot more care to put precision into our Project Proposals. As the effects of these improvements become evident, we will find other wastes that might become more important and need to be named.

I recommend every company doing lean takes this approach during their lean journey. Remember, everything in life is a process or the outcome of a process and is therefore imperfect and has waste in there. Be smart and name that waste together with your people.

This is the second "post-book" learning I wanted to give you!

The value of standard operating procedures

Patrick and I had been working together for about a year, developing the Lumen business into new areas and taking our lean culture a little higher every day, when one day, Patrick asked me to raise the standard about how we documented the Standard Work/Operating Procedures for the program, assembly, and test processes on a new product we were launching to the market – a fall detection and transmitter product for aged care settings.

Historically, if processes like these had been documented at all at Lumen, it would have been a "wall of text" that anyone except the technician who wrote it could not have possibly understood! Several times before, we had tried to set up a process to run some parts without person X present. When we dug out the SOP hidden in some folder away from the Gemba, it was unintelligible/useless as a tool. Therefore, we knew that we needed to do better if we ever wanted to scale the business at Lumen without relying on the "tribal knowledge" stuck in a few key individuals' heads.

Back to Patrick and me!

"No problem," I replied because I'd written dozens of SOPs before, particularly at my first 2 Second Lean company. I said, "No problem", even though I knew it was a pain in the *** taking photos of the process with my phone, taking notes, messing about with Excel, iteration after iteration, and so on. It often took an entire afternoon to document all but the simplest processes this way, but I thought I would "take one for the team". I already had a couple of different Standard Operation Procedure templates that I had previously developed to use as a base.

After I spent the afternoon documenting just a small part of the process, I showed the shiny new SOP to Paddy, expecting a "well done, mate!" The response was not what I expected. I got a "meh" (like my teenage daughter Cara says) and a "how long did that take?" When I told him it was the entire afternoon, Patrick asked, "Don't you have a software company?"

It was the ultimate, "Fix What Bugs You!". I took on the challenge, and by the early evening, I had sketched out the screen designs for what is now GEMBADOCS.

"GembaDocs"
https://youtu.be/ofgBlWaBuwE

"GEMBADOCS"

Tom Hughes Lumen GembaDocs Lean

Initially, we thought of the development as being for Lumen only, but when we showed it to our lean friends, the response was so positive that we built a commercial version with great success. After just one month, we already had dozens of companies around the world using the software; it was great!

We learnt so much as part of this entire process that I thought it would be good to share here because most people in lean circles do not understand how fundamental Standards/ Standard Operating Procedures are to their lean efforts.

Why Standards are important https:// youtu.be/zCVg9vl3aAA

Why standards are important

Tom Hughes Lumen GembaDocs Lean

Standard Operating Procedures are a much misunderstood and badly implemented concept in many organisations.

Business leaders often like the idea of having processes documented so that they can become less reliant on tribal knowledge, which is so easily lost, making business continuity difficult to maintain. Global staff shortages and short-term people availability shocks due to issues such as COVID restrictions exacerbate the problem.

However, these benefits are only a fraction of what well-implemented SOPs can deliver, and the fact that these benefits are underestimated is a significant reason why most businesses are not sufficiently motivated to put living, breathing, useful SOPs in place. They don't understand the benefits properly, so they don't allocate the time and resources necessary to make it happen. In addition, until now, current methods to create and maintain SOPs have been super cumbersome, meaning that most businesses don't see the effort vs reward equation stacking up.

So, to understand how this situation can be improved, let's look at some questions.

What is an SOP?

"Standard Operating Procedures are detailed descriptions of the prescribed method that team members must follow to carry out a given process in a particular organisation".

Sounds like fun, doesn't it? ☺

Here is an example of a "step by step" SOP that we generated in our GembaDocs software.

LUMEN ELECTRONICS — PreSense Assembly GD — GEMBA DOCS

1. Take front cover and place on fixture as shown. Ensure LED HOLE is bottom half!
2. Remove film from sensor. Edit.
3. Place PCB in orientation shown (ANTENNA TOP HALF) ensuring holes are aligned
4. Screw assembly x 4
5. Insert rubber seal. FLAT SURFACE UP! Ensure no fouling.
6. Insert programming cable into U7

Process Ref. No: 18
Revision: 1.004 Revision date: 24/11/2021
Date: 22/09/2021
Page 1 of 5
CYCLE TIME: 5m
Author: Tom

It sounds like we are placing a set of handcuffs on our team members rather than providing a useful tool to help them be more successful in their work.

Therein lies half the problem as to why there are so few successful SOP implementations.

For SOPs to become truly useful in an organisation, the team members need to feel that THEY OWN THEM, not that they have been imposed on them. No one likes being a slave. They need to be understood as tools that make work life easier and better, not milestones around their necks.

The key to doing this well is in our next question:

How to write an SOP?

We are very fortunate that we had a lot of interaction with a gentleman called Mark Warren around the subject of SOPs.

Mark actually WROTE THE MANUAL for how Toyota delivered standard work training in North America, called "Training within Industry".

He was super kind in helping us understand the principles better. Here is one of the posters we developed from his material because it is so often an area that people get wrong.

MAKING JOB BREAKDOWNS

1 RULE #1

Write the job breakdown where the work is done, not at your desk

2 RULE #2

Write the job breakdown as a team, not by yourself

3 RULE #3

Make sure the team include subject matter experts (the most skilled operators).

4 RULE #4

Test the job breakdown with your team. Practice to make sure it is not missing critical details and to define appropriate coaching units.

WWW.LUMEN-ELECTRONICS.COM

I know this is important from experience.

During my first ever real job back in automotive, one of my tasks was to write Standard Operating Procedures/Quality Procedures for the ISO9000 manual. It was tremendous because I learnt early on that procedures that looked great on my PC in the office, written by me, were completely useless!

During those early stages, I would proudly take out my shiny new procedure I'd written with barely any consultation with the guys doing the job and basically get told to move on! (See Rule #1 – I'm being very diplomatic in describing what they said).

I learnt that the whole process worked much better when I worked with the guys on the workplace/Gemba to document what they were already doing and then work with them to agree any changes necessary to meet the quality standard (see Rules #2, #3, and #4). They had a much higher degree of ownership when I did things that way.

When this is done as a team, each member gets to describe how they carry out the task. Often, everyone does it differently, and when this is surfaced, everyone gets to contribute and evaluate each other's method. This leads to what I call the "best of method", where the team agrees on a compilation of each member's best ways of doing a task, which is better than anyone's individual approach before. Not only does this create ownership within the team, but this process of creating a new baseline raises the standard of how that process is carried out for everyone.

This is a huge source of process improvement, which is one of the most often missed benefits of implementing SOPs. It is also a great way of building team cohesion.

In my early automotive days, I also learnt another CRUCIAL lesson that few people are truly aware of.

If you are going to create an SOP, if it ADDS burden to the people doing the job and that burden is not 100% necessary and understood, the standard will DEFINITELY not be followed. You will turn yourself into a police person trying to enforce the law all the time. It's key that the standard makes getting a high-quality outcome easier, not more difficult. Easy, simple, high-quality processes are followed. Difficult, complex processes are always a struggle.

The joys of Standard Work
https://youtu.be/VgzMrE_7Gzs

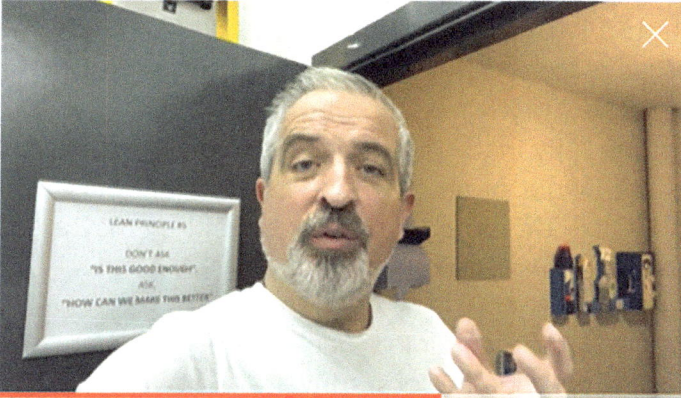

The joys of standard work

Tom Hughes Lumen GembaDocs Lean

REMEMBER THIS!

How to keep SOPs current/make sure they are followed!

SOPs can't be viewed as monuments. By that, I mean that once they are put in place, they are never supposed to move! A well-implemented SOP culture views SOPs as the baseline, the standard we all must follow.

However, there must also be a process that facilitates change and improvement.

This is most often the place where well-intentioned SOP efforts fall down.

Outdated methods, such as creating and editing in Excel, mean that adding or moving a process step turns into hours of effort, as well as managing a proper document control system to cope with revisions. These tasks often fall on one over-burdened individual who becomes the bottleneck, and eventually, people just start to bypass the system. When that happens or if there are other reasons why the process to make changes is too cumbersome, it won't be long before the SOPs just turn into **"wallpaper"**. By that, I mean that they look good, but because they are now out of date, no one is following them, and they probably provide more harm than benefit as they are a false source of security.

This particular pain point is one of the primary reasons we developed the GembaDocs software. Edits can be made in seconds, approved in minutes by the appropriate people, and put live instantaneously – all done on the Gemba by the appropriate team of people to make and approve the process change. No running backwards and forwards to a computer for hours. Minutes.

We don't know of a better way. It makes SOPs living, breathing, and useful!

Step by Step SOPs vs Video SOPs

Some organisations try to deal with SOPs by using video as a method of documenting a procedure. In the first instance, this seems like the perfect answer – it can only take minutes to shoot a video on someone's phone, right?

But then you probably need to edit it, which takes some time.

Then it needs to be hosted somewhere to be accessible to people on the Gemba, either on a server, the cloud, or a video platform like YouTube or Vimeo.

Still, it's not too bad. It's easy to document our process!

Until you want to use it as a training tool for a new starter.

For a physical process, we can watch the process together. Then we can pause it intermittently to describe it to the newbie. Now, we want to gradually move away from the newbie as they become more autonomous. Are they expected to stop/start the video to refer to it as they remind themselves of process steps? Not much fun for the newbie.

Now, what happens if we want to make a process improvement and the video needs to be revised to bring it up to date?

Where is the video stored? In many organisations that I've seen, that's a good question!

The original has probably been wiped from the originator's phone as they take up so much space. We can't edit the hosted versions on YouTube, so it's back to square one. From what I've seen, video SOPs are mostly shot once and once only, soon to become wallpaper as the actual process method evolves but the cumbersome nature of making a revision means they soon get left behind.

So, video SOPs make organisations feel good, but to question how useful they are, ask how many times they are updated. If that number is low, then the SOP is probably out of date or not much is happening in the way of process improvement!

In our organisation, some processes are on revision ten, and they have only been operating for six months. We make improvements and update our SOPs instantaneously on our GembaDocs software.

That's why we recommend step by step SOPs over video any day. In general, step by step SOPs are a better training tool, and the lack of friction involved to keep them up to date when making process improvements makes them a winning solution.

PS – on rare occasions, we integrate short videos into our step by step SOPs for nuanced processes that are tricky to describe in a step by step way. We call that a hybrid approach. GembaDocs has a facility to upload a link and display the video as a QR code on the SOP printed document. It's a rare use case, but it happens.

What kind of processes require an SOP?

We have a saying in lean circles coming from Paul Akers that "everything is a process". I would add to that by saying, "Everything is a process, and if it's a process, it can be documented and it can also be improved!"

So, any process can be documented. Here are the two key categories:

1. A core value-adding process for an organisation

The "normal" example that people consider here are often around manufacturing processes. It's true that these kinds of SOPs, especially step by step, originate from that sector. However, that's not the end of the story. Any business-critical process, particularly those key to adding value for a customer, should be documented. An organisation does not have to have a physical product for this to be the case. Think of a dentist surgery or a hospital setting, for example. There is a process from receiving/registering a patient through to myriad different forms of assessment and treatment in the process of this organisation.

So, these kinds of processes can be both physical (a manufacturing or distribution process) or virtual/computer-based.

Both will benefit from having an SOP developed to improve quality, cost, and consistency of customer experience.

2. Simple to do? Turn on a machine, change a printer cartridge, and so on.

"Put the answer where the question is!". How many times have we encountered these kinds of interruptions to the flow of our day? How do I change the paper in the printer? How do I access the Wi-Fi? How do I book in this client? And on and on. Documenting these "information deficits" on processes that can be significant productivity killers when the knowledge is not there and then making that answer available at point of use is a no-brainer improvement.

How do we make sure SOPs are followed?

When we have followed the process for writing the SOP already described, that is a big step towards ensuring that the people actually doing the job feel ownership for the SOP and are therefore likely to follow it, but on its own, this is unlikely to be enough.

It is key that everyone who carries out "task X" is trained in how to do it as per the SOP. This is especially important for business-critical, value-adding processes.

This was another key part of the learning we received from Mark.

We developed this graphic based on his material.

The bottom line of this graphic is the most important. **"If the person hasn't learned, the instructor hasn't taught".**

In my experience, very few organisations outside of automotive truly understand this. It's generally the exact opposite!

So, preparing the worker (Step 1) and presenting the operation (Step 2) in a manner where they clearly understand why each step is necessary and the key points to look out for is the responsibility of the INSTRUCTOR. Trying out the newbie's performance (Step 3) so that the INSTRUCTOR validates the understanding and performance of the newbie before they put them on their own (Step 4) and then ensuring that they get adequately supported before tapering off the coaching is key.

For the vast majority of processes, if the newbie doesn't get it, it's likely the process is unclear, too complex or burdensome, or the instructor has not done Steps 1 – 3 properly. It's a true case of "attack the process, not the person".

Failure in this area is a key reason why so many businesses have a problem with a "churn" of new starters who do not stay long in the business while creating a huge burden on the long-term team members who constantly have to support the new starts, causing further reductions in productivity because they aren't actually adding value.

It's a great example where "pulling the andon" and understanding the root causes of the problem really helps. Very often, the problems lie in these areas – poorly documented standards and training processes – that stress out the new starts and the existing long-term people alike. Management needs to understand this and support a change in approach. The results can be miraculous.

So, training is evidently key, but it doesn't just end there.

How to access Standard Operating Procedures

How team members can access the SOPs is also important. How often have we seen work instructions, how to's, or manuals put into a file and then stored away in some drawer or cupboard just to gather dust? Hardly a way for them to live, breathe, and be useful standards within an organisation!

So, no matter the SOP, it's key that the standard is easily accessible at point of use and that all relevant team members know how to access them.

SOPs can be made accessible in the following ways:

1. Printed out and displayed in full
2. A QR code that can be scanned by a mobile device to display the SOP. This can also be put onto applicable

process documentation and automated within an ERP system

3. A "lean bible" where SOPs can be accessed via URL links for reference

4. Via mobile/desktop application when they have been generated with specific software (e.g., GembaDocs)

The appropriate method depends on the application. Incidentally, we designed the GembaDocs software to have "always the latest" URLs, meaning that if they are kept in a lean bible or ERP system, the URL when clicked/QR code when scanned will always display the latest version of the SOP without the user/administrator needing to do anything else. How cool is that?!

But let's look at why we would bother doing any of this.

Why are Standard Operating Procedures important?

The diagram shows my now favourite lean quotation of all time from Taiichi Ohno, the "Father of Lean": "Without standards, there can be no improvement".

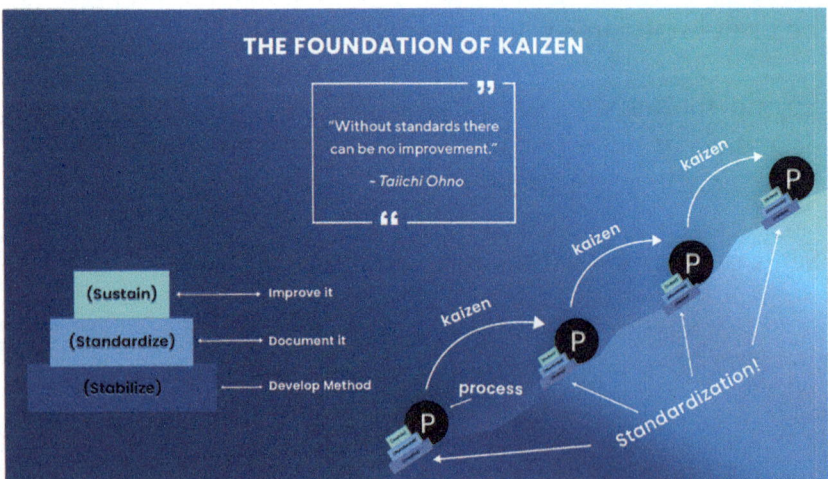

THE FOUNDATION OF KAIZEN

"Without standards there can be no improvement."
- Taiichi Ohno

(Sustain) ← Improve it
(Standardize) ← Document it
(Stabilize) — Develop Method

kaizen
process
standardization!

Why would Taiichi make such a bold proclamation?

It's because of that slippery slope between the bottom of the slope shown here, which represents where most companies are, with no standards (SOPs), no documented processes at all or, just as bad, what I call "wallpaper" standards that aren't kept up to date and that no one is using or following. Still, management divorced from the Gemba get to think they have SOPs in place when clearly, to any objective view, they do not!

We created the GembaDocs software to reduce the burden of this "develop – document – improve" process, making it possible to create or edit Standard Operating Procedures within minutes, not hours or days. It really is a gamechanger, making it possible to create and maintain those "backstops" that prevents the solid ball of your process from rolling down the quality, cost and customer experience hill!

This next diagram makes it even more clear that standards are literally the "foundation of lean".

GEMBA DOCS

CUSTOMER SATISFACTION
BUSINESS SUCCESS

JIT	Respect for People	JIDOKA
Pull	Team Building	Poka-yoke
Flow	Empowerment	Andon
Takt Time	Cross Training	Autonomation
Heijunka	Hoshin	5 Whys
Cell Design	Supplier Relationships	Line Stops
SMED		Built in Quality

STABILITY and STANDARDIZATION

55	Standard Operations
TPM	Kaizen

This schematic is often used to demonstrate the Toyota Production System, represented as a "House Of Lean" with Customer Satisfaction and Business Success as the apex of the roof, supported by the pillars of Just In Time, Respect for People (Culture) and Jidoka techniques. **The foundation of the temple is "Stability and Standardisation",** with Standard Operation/Standard Operating Procedures as one of those key principles.

When I hold training workshops for GembaDocs customers, one of the lines I always use is, "You can have all the culture you want, but without stability and standardisation, your lean efforts are built on sand."

It is that important.

Adding an improvement to that chaos is just adding another variation that will likely stay in place for a day or two by just some of the people carrying out the process, then disappear.

Lean guru Masaaki Imai, founder of the Kaizen Institute, describes this phenomenon better than I ever could!

"It is impossible to improve any process until it is standardized. If the process is shifting from here to there, then any improvement will just be one more variation that is occasionally used and mostly ignored. One must standardize, and thus stabilize the process, before continuous improvement can be made."

- MASAAKI IMAI

LOVE EXPANDS

How often have you or your team made a great change to a process, only to come back a few days later to find out that no one is following it? That can be very frustrating.

That's why having a clear process of how the Standard Operating Procedures (as we examined in "How to write an SOP") are documented is key.

Benefits of Standard Operating Procedures

When we talk about benefits here, we are talking about when SOPs are done right! That can only be achieved when the concept is well understood by all stakeholders in the organisation and the appropriate tools and resources are allocated to the SOP effort.

1. A massive source of improvement

   Firstly, the initial "best of" approach becomes the baseline for how process X is done.

   Secondly, making process improvements on a solid foundation means they are much more likely to stick than adding another variation to an already unstable process.

2. Reduce stress for team members

   There is a clear way of executing all tasks for everyone. Minimise planning hassles caused by absentees or people leaving the business. Well-implemented SOPs also ensure business continuity.

3. Reduce people churn

   SOPs provide a consistent basis for training. New starts get adequate support to integrate into the organisation with the SOPs as their reference.

4. Process stability

   When team members "own" their already improved process and that SOP is consistently followed by EVERYONE, it leads to less variation in the process outcome, which can often be measured in terms of quality, cost, or customer experience. Overall, less waste!

If you'd like to learn more about SOPs, the GembaDocs software, and how can they can be integrated into your organisation culture, feel free to drop me a line on my contact details at the end of the book.

So overall, to conclude, one thing about lean is...

You will never stop learning. It is actually a really important "fifth step" that I think it's great to consciously state beyond just being consistent and reviewing your kata. We always need to be raising the bar and deepening our own knowledge, primarily as individuals but also as the collective.

Everyone I know who has truly got the "lean bug" is crazy about learning. I even coined a bad joke: **"Lean is spelt wrong. It should be spelt leaRn!"**

If you're going to make your lean efforts sustainable in the long run, embracing new learning for yourself (learning certainly starts with I!), leading by example and encouraging your entire team is key.

AND JUST BEFORE I GO!

We looked at our "5 C's" of Candour, Commitment, Coaching, Consistency, and Continuous Learning in a sequential way, which is good for an organisation at the beginning of its lean journey. However, they are also a set of "values" that need to be cultivated in an organisation for lean to SUSTAIN and as has been the message throughout this book, that "starts with I".

So, everyone, every day, exhibiting Candour – Stop, Speak Up, Listen, and Act.

Everyone, every day, not just the leadership team walking the talk of Commitment to excellence.

Realising that we all have the opportunity and obligation to be coaches within our organisation, especially the senior people, but also every single person can be a coach to others.

Exhibiting Consistency by doing the simple things right. Giving ourselves to the process of the Morning Meeting, turning up no matter what and making those simple improvements to make life better every day.

Coaching with Triple X behaviours, not just people with big job titles. Everyone.

Knowing that this is never going to stop. That we all as individuals are giving ourselves to a process of Continuous Learning. Continuous development of ourselves and our team.

Everyone. Every Day. Engaged!

So, to sign off for now, as we say in Ireland, "Keep 'er lit!" and **GOOD LUCK ON YOUR LEAN JOURNEY.**

I hope you enjoyed reading this book every bit as much as I enjoyed writing it.

If you embrace it, lean can change your life in an extremely positive way. I know that because that is what it has done for me, both personally and professionally, and I am very proud to be a part of this community.

For those of you that might be interested in working with me as a formal coach to support your organisation, or who would simply just like some help on your Lean journey, you can find ways to connect with me at the start of this book, you can drop me a line on WhatsApp, Signal, or Voxer on +44 (0) 7712 133615. I will be delighted to help in any way I can.

There are few things in life that bring me so much joy as being able to devote time to helping more companies come on to this amazing path. I would be delighted to hear from you.

I am also open to Non-Executive roles in companies that want to do truly great things. I believe that most organisations do not bring in enough of an outside perspective to stimulate new thinking and that this leaves them vulnerable to stagnation and competitive shifts. My time at Olaer provided me with great experience around this, so if that resonates, also feel free to get in touch.

So for now, all the best in your positive endeavours and God Bless!

Tom

- Lean is meant to be flexible. Adapt the principles to work for YOUR business.
- Standards are the foundation of lean. Without them, your efforts are built on sand.
- **If you really love lean, you will never stop leaRning!**

Made in the USA
Las Vegas, NV
05 July 2022

51130243R10115